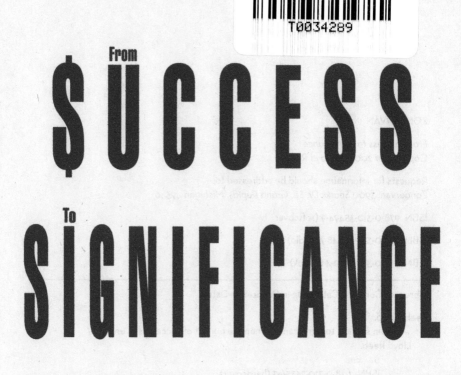

From
$UCCESS
To
$IGNIFICANCE

When the Pursuit of Success Isn't Enough

Lloyd Reeb

ZONDERVAN®

ZONDERVAN

From Success to Significance
Copyright © 2004 by Lloyd Reeb

Requests for information should be addressed to:
Zondervan, 3900 *Sparks Dr. SE, Grand Rapids, Michigan* 49546

ISBN 978-0-310-35494-9 (softcover)

ISBN 978-0-310-30448-7 (audio)

ISBN 978-0-310-31781-4 (ebook)

Library of Congress Cataloging-in-Publication Data

Reeb, Lloyd.
    From success to significance: when the pursuit of success isn't enough /
Lloyd Reeb.
        p. cm.
        ISBN 978-0-310-25356-3 (hardcover)
    1. Middle aged persons—Religious life. 2. Middle aged persons—Psychology.
3. Self-realization—Religious aspects—Christianity. I. Title.
BV4579.5.R44   2004
248.8′4—dc22   2004011984

Cover design: *Jeff Gifford*
Interior design: *Michelle Espinoza*

First printing December 2017 / Printed in the United States of America

From $UCCESS
To $IGNIFICANCE

I would like to express my deepest appreciation to my friend and mentor Bob Buford, the author of Halftime, *whose authentic, sacrificial life, and deep love for Jesus Christ has inspired me and thousands of other successful leaders at midlife to pursue eternal significance in our second half.*

Thanks to Linda, my beautiful wife, who for more than twenty-five years has lived out for me what it really means to follow Christ in everyday life.

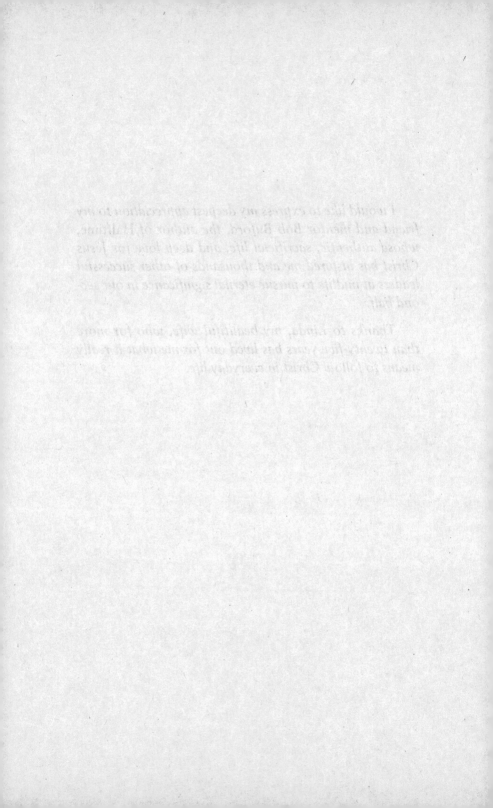

Contents

PART III: IMPORTANT MIDLIFE ISSUES I NEVER DREAMED OF

Foreword by Bob Buford

Let me begin by confessing the intent of this foreword right up front. My hope for Lloyd Reeb's book, which you now hold, is that it will convince you of two things—the first is that the change-of-life season described as Halftime is nearly universal in the developed world and critical to Halftimers. The second is that the transition from success to significance as a central motive force in life's second half is not at all dependent upon income and net worth.

Lloyd has captured ideas and illustrations that will enable almost everyone who desires it to engage their passions in a life of significance. This can be done either alongside their primary work life in a parallel career, or as a primary career of work, serving others in which money making takes a necessary but subordinate role.

As the author of the book Halftime, I told my own particular and unique story, which happens to be that of a multimillionaire, and the question always comes up: "Is Halftime a rich, white, male thing?" This question seems to float in the air in conversations at the Halftime Workshops that Lloyd and I have done around the United States.

The answer is "No, it's not," but that always takes some explanation. Mine is a story of having the good fortune of beginning in the right business (television broadcasting, then cable television) at the right time (the sixties to the nineties), in the right place (the US). It is an example of one Halftime opportunity in the twentieth-first century. But my story is only one of millions (yes, millions!). The Halftime stories are many and diverse—as diverse as people can be in an individualistic time and place like ours.

The great creation of the nineteenth and especially the twentieth century has been the middle class. That's my story and that is Lloyd's story too. The main difference is that my story of successful commercial activity runs about twenty years of steady and fairly intense compounding longer than his. I'm sixty-four. Lloyd is forty-two. He was and still is in a different form of business than I (senior-focused real estate), and he caught on to the parallel-career idea sooner that I did. But his story shows the path from success to significance just as clearly as mine does. That's why I encouraged him to write this book. That plus the fact that there's probably nobody else who has sat across from more Halftimers than Lloyd, and his story at his age is more representative of forty-something stories than mine now is.

Now let me make one more point. There's a burgeoning new field of research and writing that shows conclusively that there is no connection between money and happiness. None! Not positive or negative. Zero! A terrific new book, The Progress Paradox (2003), rolls up most of the prior research and is currently making its way up the bestseller lists. It, among others, contains these three assertions, which I quote:

1. [There is a] "revolution of satisfied expectations," the uneasy feeling that accompanies actually receiving the things that you dreamed of.
2. That society is undergoing a fundamental shift from "material want" to "meaning want," with ever larger numbers of people reasonably secure in terms of living standards, but feeling they lack significance in their lives. A transition from "material want" to "meaning want" is not a prediction that men and women will cease being materialistic; no social indicator points to such a possibility. It is a prediction that ever more millions will expect both pleasant living standards and a broad sense that their lives possess purpose. This is a conundrum, as meaning is much more difficult to acquire than material possessions.

3. That new psychological research, which seeks to explain why some are happy and others not, suggests it is in your self-interest to be forgiving, grateful, and optimistic—that these presumptively altruistic qualities are actually "essential to personal well-being."[1]

Significance is an existential need, not an economic need. Summing up the field: Nearly all well-being research supports the basic conclusion that money and material needs are only weakly associated with leading a good life. The magic number at which money decouples from happiness is far less than you might think. In fact some research suggests it may be as low as about $40,000 for a family of four.

My basic logic and Lloyd's too, as you will discover as you read his account, goes like this: Why trade that which you can't acquire enough of (significance) for that which you have plenty of already (success)? All of us will face a final exam when we arrive at Heaven's Gate for the beginning of our new life. As I visualize it, there will be two questions: (1) "What did you do about Jesus?" and (2) "What did you do with what I gave you to work with?"

The book you are about to read is like getting the right answers before the exam. A pretty good deal.

And not a moment too soon.

Bob Buford
Author, *Halftime: Changing Your Game Plan from Success to Significance*
Founder, Leadership Network
www.halftime.org

Introduction

Ten years ago I made a midlife decision to reorient my life
toward significance. Now I no longer have that sick feeling in
my stomach of being trapped in a life of busyness, pursuing
things that won't last at the expense of things I value most.
Strangely, though I work just as hard as ever, I feel little stress,
especially when compared to the gut-wrenching stress I experienced as a real estate developer in the first half of my life. I'm
free of the rat race.

I remember those sleepless nights, rolling around in bed,
wondering if the bank would fund my next deal and whether
demand for my seniors' housing project would be as strong as
I predicted. I remember the anxiety of thinking I was wasting
my life chasing illusions, secretly asking myself if this is what I
was created to do.

Sure, I still worry from time to time—when the stock mar-
kets fluctuate or unexpected family expenses emerge. But it's a
different kind of worry. I still enjoy working hard, reaching
goals, and taking risks; but today I do it out of a sense of calling rather than some unexplained inner drivenness. I do it with
the confidence that I'm in the "sweet spot" of what I was created to do. And I'm having the time of my life. I wake up every
morning feeling lucky to know what I'm passionate about. I
know the things I'm good at, and I've been given the gift of
being able to focus my life on them.

I made that "Halftime" transition in 1993. I pushed the
pause button in the middle of the game of life so that I might
look back on the lessons and accomplishments of the first half,
to reflect on what will really matter in the long run, and then to
redirect my life in the second half. Specifically, I wanted to pursue the possibility of moving from success to significance. But

without millions of dollars in the bank, I knew it would take creativity and intention to discover how to pursue significance.

How I made this transition, mistakes and all, is the subject of this book. Hundreds of thousands of people have read Bob Buford's book *Halftime* and felt touched with a longing for the kind of significance he describes there. But many readers—regular, everyday people like you and I—have said, "That's great for Bob, but how can I do that without being wealthy?"

When I first met Bob, I described my own difficult transition. Without hesitation he looked me in the eyes and said, "Just maybe God pulled you through that knothole so that you could invest your life in helping others avoid it." And that is what I am dedicating my life to now.

Each day, between ten and twelve thousand people in the United States turn fifty. One in four Americans are over fifty, and the fifty-to-sixty-four-year-old age group is expected to grow by 50 percent by 2015, making the mature consumer market one that demands attention. But how many of those people focus on their longing for significance?

Of the millions entering midlife, a growing number are charting a Halftime course, choosing to swim upstream in our culture, away from the temporary toward the eternal, simplifying their lives so they can focus on the things that really matter. This book recounts my own life story as well as the experiences and insights of others who have also made this journey. This book will ask tough questions and point you to resources that will enable you to redefine success and pursue significance—and chart a new course for your second half.

I didn't sell my business or quit my job. Instead, I redefined success, reallocated my energies, and re-prioritized my family's spending. I cut the time I spent doing business, found a niche as one of the pastors at a large church in Charlotte, North Carolina, and help high-capacity business people find their second-half calling. As a result, my wife, Linda, and I have had more time over the past decade to spend with our three kids as they grow, time to spend together playing tennis and sailing. I have enjoyed getting back into good physical shape and building a few close friendships. By allocating part of my week to ministry, I've had the thrill of being a part of many men's and women's spiritual journeys as they pursue God and explore their personal faith, and I have traveled around the world on mission trips. I feel blessed to have had the freedom to invest a good part of my life in things that I believe have eternal significance.

Do you know the most interesting thing about all this? What makes all this possible is not that I'm rich, smart, or lucky. What makes my life today so different from the lives of typical forty-something executives has been choices, not chance. It's about options, not affluence; about availability more than ability. I'm not downplaying the thrill or value of success. Instead, I'm recommending that you build on the success of your first half of life and transform it into significance.

At times I wanted to forget all about making a difference and simply go back to making money. I knew how to do it, and I could measure my effectiveness in dollars and cents. At times I was angry at the apparent lack of urgency within the nonprofit organizations I was trying to help. After all, intensity and urgency were keys to my success in real estate development—and that was done strictly for the money. So, since this new work was all about helping people, changing their lives and perhaps even their eternal destinies, why did these nonprofit organizations seem so unfocused? Why did they seem to have far less urgency than my partner and I had in our business? Why did some of the staff saunter out of the office at 4:30 p.m.?

But I soon realized that part of the burden was with me. I hadn't yet learned how to measure effectiveness in the nonprofit arena of helping others.

Yet, despite all this, I would never want to return to my old life, to the time before my midlife transition when I pursued success with little regard for eternal significance.

PART I

FINDING THE FREEDOM TO DREAM AT MIDLIFE

Chapter 1

My Two-Minute Warning:
A Life-Defining Moment

The shadows casting down the brick wall created the warmth and richness of a building that I felt sure seniors would love to call home for many years to come. The Georgian-style building overlooked a beautiful bend in the Tay River and incorporated all the conveniences of comfortable, modern living. We named it Huntington Green. It was our most beautiful housing development to date, and it represented the culmination of months of intense planning and work.

Like a sculptor, I stood back and reflected on this finished work, which had once been nothing more than a vision in my mind. It was ribbon-cutting day, but for me it was so much more. It was the confirmation I needed that I should invest my life in something more significant than simply creating beautiful buildings and making money.

I had just returned from five weeks in Albania, where I not only saw poverty and despair everywhere I looked but had the opportunity to work side-by-side with people who brought hope and help to this country in turmoil. With the fall of many communist governments in Eastern Europe in the early 1990s, Albania remained the most staunchly communist country in the world, as well as the most isolated. The country's communist experiment had left it impoverished. Its three million people depended on ancient farming methods, resulting in a tragically inefficient agricultural industry that was unable to compete in a global economy. After decades of centrally planned farming, the Albanian farmers had no idea how to plan their own crops, assess costs, set prices, or market their product.

Finally, the old regime fell. Within months, the new Albanian government recognized the critical importance of retraining the country's farmers. Creative, entrepreneurial leaders with SEND International, a nonprofit missionary agency, rose to the challenge and offered to send dozens of successful American and Canadian farmers to Albania, to volunteer their time to help Albanian farmers one-on-one. SEND International asked me to lead the project.

I felt underequipped to lead such a project. After all, I didn's even know where Albania was, and I knew nothing about farming. But I did know that my leadership skills had proven themselves in the marketplace and that I desperately wanted to find an avenue to make my life count for something more than making money—to be a part of something bigger than myself.

So, at the invitation of the Albanian government, we took more than seventy farmers to teach the Albanians the basics of farming in a market economy. As they hung out together over two weeks, the Albanians wanted to learn more about our Western farms, our families, and even our faith in God. For me, this project was a first step toward answering the deep longing of my heart for significance.

Each team spent two weeks in their assigned village, working with every farmer that showed any receptivity. They lived in the farmers' homes—cement-block houses crowded together along mud roads, with no phones and animals everywhere. Farmland surrounded each village, and each morning the farmers walked out to their fields carrying their rustic tools with them. They did most of their work by hand. Their homes were cold and dirty, with no indoor plumbing. The typical Albanian farmer owned just a handful of acres, a few chickens, and a cow.

Our Canadian and American farmers, by contrast, owned hundreds of acres and had huge tractors, trucks, and harvesting equipment—and yet they humbly built a bridge of trust with each Albanian family, opening the door to deeper conversation. Often their discussion moved beyond farming to family, politics, and even spiritual topics.

The Albanians' hearts overflowed with spiritual questions. After all, for more than seventy years they had been told that God did not exist. But even as they looked around at the beauty and complexity of nature, they questioned that idea.

I will never forget how this experience affected one sixty-year-old hog farmer from Tennessee, named Burress Nichols, as well as a fifty-year-old turkey farmer from Vancouver, named Ron Heppel. These busy, successful farmers had paid their own way to Albania to give two weeks of their time. Even while they recovered from jet lag and culture shock, they worked day and night to help dozens of farmers rethink their farming strategies. They slept on old, musty beds, used smelly outhouses—and, at the end of their time, openly cried as they gave their host families good-bye hugs. The entire village came out to say farewell. Burress and Ron had fallen in love with these people and felt awed by the real help and hope they were able to bring.

Burress and Ron had everything in life: loving families, the latest farm equipment, large homes, nice cars, respect in their communities, deep relationships with God—and yet they cried as they left. Why? What had touched their hearts so deeply? How is it possible that all of us had had such a rewarding experience in such an awful place?

Those questions were in the back of my mind as I prepared to join the ribbon-cutting ceremony for our new building. Everyone was there: the mayor and local media, contractors and new residents. The contrast between the two worlds was all too clear to me.

The bright yellow ribbon stretched between the main pillars of the entrance, and cameras captured the moment. Ribbon cuttings always feel like a birth and graduation all rolled into one. It's the beginning of something and the end at the same time. As my partner and I stood in front of the last building we would ever build together—our most beautiful and profitable real estate development ever—I sensed that a new birth was taking place in my life. Even as I spoke to the group, my thoughts wandered and I felt a stirring in my heart. Recently I watched a videotape of that event, filmed by a local TV station, and from that perspective, nothing spectacular seemed to be going on. But for me, it was a defining moment.

In the language of the National Football League, this was my two-minute warning. Just before halftime, officials stop the game to make sure that both sides know that two minutes remain before the halftime break. I thought of this as one of the kairos moments in my life (the Greek word *kairos* means "the right, proper, or favorable time"), and I knew a new phase of life was appearing on the horizon in my life and the life of my family.

As I stood at the ribbon cutting, I felt I could almost hear the bulldozers one hundred years from now pushing the building into a great pile to make way for something new, something to replace what we had worked so hard to create. I felt that within a hundred years this building would either be torn down or become a rundown tenement in a "bad section of town." Did I want to invest my entire life in developing buildings that would only be torn down?

You too may have your own *kairos* moment, perhaps when you realize you are spending too many precious hours in meetings, or perhaps when you've tackled yet another urgent project, only to have it canceled or altered because of a merger. Perhaps you spend your time solving major issues, which, in the long run, are relatively insignificant.

This morning, at a coffee shop, my friend Rob told me that he could easily continue growing his company at exponential rates, but he also knows in the end it will be just like Monopoly: "All the pieces go back in the box." Many of us spend much of our time driving the next quarter's earnings, even while our potential impact on eternity slips past us on all sides.

At the ribbon-cutting ceremony, my mind kept flashing back to Albania, to the farm families in those remote villages; to the old ladies with wrinkled faces and eyes filled with despair; to the teens whose hopes and dreams seemed so unlikely because of the wretched economy; to the fathers who felt the heavy burden of providing for their families' needs and safety when ethnic war seemed inevitable. I thought about the hope we were able to bring them, not just for farming, but also for eternity. We brought them the wonderful story of a loving God who sends people to serve them when they are in need and who offers forgiveness to all. Many of them felt it was like offering cool water to a friend in the heat of the summer on a dry and dusty road.

It dawned on me that, if this whole Christian thing is real and true, then in one hundred years, when our buildings are getting torn down, those farmers will just be starting to enjoy what God has in store for them for an eternity in heaven. Eternity is a very long time, and the impact we have on someone's eternity seems to overpower even the most noble benefits we can bring them in the seventy some years they live on this earth.

But wait, my mind argued, *these seniors' buildings are about serving people too. These developments contribute to society. They provide a platform for us to share our faith among people who are late in life. Aren't we living out the Christ-life to the degree that we can reflect Jesus in our interactions with contractors and residents, architects and bankers?*

Valid points. Of course, I knew I could be doing a much better job than I was at reflecting the character of God through my business. But even if I reached some pinnacle of witness in the marketplace, I still felt a sense of loss to invest such a high percentage of my time and leadership ability in something that eventually would cease to exist.

Several questions turned over in my mind:

- Is there more to life than just this?
- Is being an ethical leader in the marketplace enough?
- Could I really make a significant difference in people's lives by taking an active role in service to others, or should I focus on making money and giving financially to support the work of others?
- Given all the obligations in my life, such as my marriage, family, work, and maintaining our chosen lifestyle, how

could I possibly create enough space in life to pursue significance?

At a deep level, I knew that my own identity was defined by being a successful real estate developer, and I wondered what kind of identity I would have if I reoriented my life toward some more "noble" cause. I began to think seriously about how equally "noble" it might be for a person to follow God's lead to be salt and light in the business world.

People at this stage of life often ask such questions. In his book on this topic, Bob Buford labeled this phase of life "Halftime." He provided the vernacular and permission for hundreds of thousands of us to address what we are feeling.

Halftime is a pause in the middle of the game of life to reflect on our first half—who we have become—and to discover what we want at the end of life and to redirect our time, talent, and treasure toward something significant. For some, Halftime comes when facing retirement; for me, it came a bit earlier.

I asked a veteran NFL coach to explain what really happens in the locker room during the halftime break. His insights provide a framework for us as we unpack the Halftime journey. He summarizes the most effective halftime as a brief look at:

1. what we did right in the first half
2. what we did wrong
3. what we need to change
4. what we are going to do to change it

Most importantly, halftime provides an opportunity for the team to gain a new focus for the second half and the confidence and passion to go out again and give it all they have.

That's exactly what Halftime was for me, and what it has been for tens of thousands of others.

Halftime is not just for the rich, however. It's not about bailing out of corporate America or selling your company. It's not just a male thing. Many women go through Halftime, including those who were successful in a career as well as those who choose to focus on raising a family for a first-half focus—and many of the issues are the same.

Nor is it even just a Christian thing. It is a generational and cultural phenomenon. For those of us whose lives are based in faith, these questions have an eternal perspective. For Christians, Halftime is about our impact on eternity and discovering what we were created to do.

The generation now turning fifty is the healthiest, wealthiest, and best-educated generation ever to reach midlife. Its members have many productive years ahead. Many who have reflected on their lives recall that they were the generation who wanted to change the world, but they often find themselves mired in pursuit of other things.

Historically, only a fraction of the world has had the luxury of pausing at midlife to rethink where they are going and to alter their direction. Most people in previous generations had no flexibility to change what they did for a living. When we study the lives of some of the most significant leaders in American history, however, we find surprising examples of Halftime experiences.

In his late forties, Thomas Jefferson began to wonder what would make the second half of his life significant. He had invested his first forty-five years in his country, to the neglect of his family and the passion of his heart, farming. In his first half he played a pivotal role in the formation of America, built his estate, Monticello, cultivated his mind, and gained national influence in the newly formed country. After his wife, Martha, passed away, Jefferson deeply grieved his loss. He sought to be the best father he could to his daughters but felt pulled throughout their teen years between his commitments to country and family. His time in Paris gave birth to a new perspective on life that began the midlife thought process. He had tasted success and now his soul longed for something deeper and richer. Something perhaps more lasting.

Jefferson celebrated his fiftieth birthday by packing up his books and furniture and sending them from Philadelphia, where Congress met, back to Monticello. It was time for a new approach at midlife. He describes his Halftime experience in a remarkable letter to James Madison on February 27, 1793: "The motion of my blood no longer keeps time with the tumult of the world. It leads me to seek for happiness in the lap and love of my family, in the society of my neighbors and my books, in the wholesome occupations of my farm and my affairs, in an interest or affection in every bud that opens, in every breath that blows around me."

As he reflected on his first-half work, he described himself as "worn down with labors from morning to night, and day to day, knowing them as fruitless to others as they are vexations to myself . . . cut off from my family and friends, my affairs abandoned to chaos and derangement, in short giving everything I love in exchange for everything I hate." While Jefferson was one of the few in his day who had options about how he would invest the second half of his life, his heart journey seems remarkably similar to the one many of us travel today.

You are among millions with similar midlife questions. I remember wondering, "What options do I really have? How can I arrange my life so that I can tackle whatever God has for me that uses my gifts and passions to make the greatest possible impact with my life?"[1]

I told Andrew Mitton, who was both my business partner and closest friend, "I can't continue to focus all of my energy on developing these buildings. I need to pursue whatever it is that God's doing in my heart."

Andrew is a quiet but deep thinking man whose analytical mind and consistent, tenacious character were probably the largest contributing factors to our business success. I felt as if I were letting him down as I spoke. My part of the partnership was critical, and if God called me to allocate my time in a different direction, it would affect him just as much as it would affect me. But I thought I would be disobeying God if I kept silent. I wasn't sure how he would react.

Andrew's quiet assurance that if God was moving me in a different direction, it would be okay with him proved to be a critical part of my journey. Since then, as I have helped hundreds of others take a similar journey from success to significance, I have learned just how important it is to *not* take this journey alone.

I felt sure of one thing, though: I had to have a single focus in my life and I needed to decide if that would be success or significance. The Bible, in its usual profound way, says that "a double minded" person is unstable in everything he does (James 1). It seemed clear to me that I would need to decide what would drive how I allocated my time, talent, and treasure, and that if I did not decide, I would vacillate between success and significance.

I feared that if I chose significance over success, my decision would strip all of the adrenaline, adventure, and passion out of my life. Second, I wondered how we would handle the financial implications for our family.

Since then I have discovered that neither of these underlying issues are "show stoppers." Instead of finding my passion and my identity stripped away, to my surprise, I have been given freedom to build on the passions God instilled in my heart and to ultimately redefine my identity.

Your Two-Minute Warning

What in your life is turning your heart toward greater significance? Perhaps a birthday, a traumatic event, the death of a loved one, a divorce, or a financial setback. Or has recent success caused you to wonder if there is life after achieving the financial goals you set in your twenties?

Chris, a friend of mine, was recently promoted to senior vice president of a bank. He ordered his new silver BMW and soon after it arrived, he realized that he too had arrived where he had been headed his whole career—but something seemed missing. That began a journey that, less than a year later, finds him still pushing hard at the bank, but also dedicating ten hours of his week to help hundreds of African children orphaned by AIDS. His heart today overflows with fulfillment, both in his work at the bank (which he does for God's honor) and in the privilege of helping even one orphan kid in Africa.

What factors about your current work are causing you to pause and redefine success? Do you sense that if you left your job, the team would go on just the same? Have you sensed an emptiness after new promotions or after landing a new client?

How have you defined success during the first half of life? Take a minute and write down your first half definition of success.

Now let's take a look at the journey that led me to the defining moment at the ribbon-cutting ceremony.

Chapter 2

Redefining Success—
from a First-Quarter Perspective

The first quarter of life shapes us more than any other period. In our first twenty years, the core values of our heart are formed, affecting every decision we make. People in our world, their goals and dreams, what they model for us, shape us in ways we do not know at the time (and to which they are often oblivious). I based my own view of success on values I picked up early in life.

At Halftime I had to come to grips with those core values. I had to ask myself whether they were based in reality, if they were true and healthy. And then to redefine success and build my second half intentionally around a few core values I really believed in.

I grew up in suburban Philadelphia, in a middle-income family with three brothers. My grandparents emigrated from the Alsace region of France at the turn of the nineteenth century and lived in a small house. My grandfather worked in a noisy factory. He and his family rode the trolley because they did not own a car. They never took a family vacation.

As a boy, I simply could not relate to their world. I lived in a new world because my dad worked hard to lift himself up out of his parents' world. He paid his own way through college, became the first of the family to own a car, and got a job in management.

In his pursuit of success, he took the "early bird" train downtown to the office, leaving before sunrise on the 6:05 a.m. train, dressed in a spotless navy blue three-piece suit, black polished shoes, and white pressed shirt—with gold cuff links, of course. Long before we woke up, he would come into our room and kiss my brother and me good-bye. I can still remember the smell of his aftershave lotion as he leaned over my bed. Later I would hear the "early bird" whistle blow as Dad's train was leaving the station several miles away. It seemed to mark in my mind the beginning of another day and the commitment of a hard-working dad, that he would continue to provide for his family. But it also made me wonder what was out there that was so valuable to warrant such a focused pursuit.

Part of me felt drawn to what I saw of Dad's corporate life—the corner office, the fascinating projects, and the sense of satisfaction so evident in his demeanor as he talked about his work. I remember walking into his office as a little boy and feeling how big it seemed, with the beautiful furniture, soft leather chairs, a photo of me on the credenza. Everything looked organized and made me feel he had things in control. It was clear how his faith integrated into his work. I admired him and his drive. I admired his determination to rise above his parents' economic level. He often talked about what it takes to succeed. He highlighted the value of dressing for success.

As early as my teens and through my twenties, I had a clearly defined understanding of what a successful life looks like. I had seen it modeled by many successful people whom I admired. I summed it up this way:

You work hard

- to get into the best college
- to launch into the best career
- to make the most money
- to accumulate the most toys
- to retire as early as possible

This definition of success was exciting and enticing to me because I knew clearly where I was going. I could measure my progress all along the way. My grades, the college I got into, the money I accumulated—all were so easily measurable. It was comforting to know the plan. I felt satisfaction in winning. What on earth I would do when I retired early, or how fulfilling that would feel, never garnered a single thought.

Sure, the first half of my life was infused with small elements of service to others, above and beyond reaching for success: things like a commitment to my wife and young family, and time spent volunteering with our church youth group. But now, as I look back from my second-half perspective, I see that I had no sense of "calling" in my original definition of success. No sense of a Creator God who just might know what was best for me or have a specific plan for my life. I had no understanding of the passions hardwired into my heart. Rather, I lived by an oversimplified, two-dimensional, linear understanding of what a meaningful life should look like.

My first-half definition of success, lived out to its fullest extent, would cause me to spend my life reaching financial and material goals, accomplishing tasks, and solving problems—but I would never get in touch with my soul, with how God created me. I might never discover a higher reason to live beyond the confines of accumulating things.

As Bob Buford says, "Our first half is about how to make a living, and our second half has the promise of being about how to make a life."

Beneath the surface, however, my heart was never entirely satisfied with that pursuit of success. Even as I planned for college and career, whenever I heard the "early bird" train whistle blow, I sensed something important was missing. When I saw firsthand all the other businessmen caught up in the whole navy-suit/dress-for-success thing, I wondered if there just might be more to life than reaching another year's quota or moving up to the next rung on the company ladder.

For many people, just getting to that next rung can trigger the beginning of Halftime in their lives. For me it began when my first real estate project earned surprising success, and for the first time in my life, it dawned on me that everything I would ever acquire actually belonged to God. Everything was simply on loan to me for just a short time. My skills, my assets, my influence, and each day I remained alive and breathing were simply entrusted to me temporarily. God's desire was that I invest those things wisely, to yield eternal dividends. When the light of this idea first shined on my heart, it brought a sense of awesome responsibility combined with a feeling of exhilarating opportunity.

I had purchased a scenic apple orchard planted on rolling hills, located just on the outskirts of the city. I dreamed of building a subdivision of large homes on spacious lots served by a winding road. But the odds seemed stacked against it. The county planning commission already had said that it would not approve such a development. Beyond that, the engineering design, earthwork, sewers, curbs, and road would cost hundreds of thousands of dollars. What made it even more unlikely was that I was just twenty-two years old and earning very little at my first job in the marketing department of a bank.

Day after day, as the project ultimately became a successful reality, I could see God's hand unmistakably at work. When all the dust settled, the orchard had literally become a beautiful new neighborhood. Why, against all odds, had the project been approved? Why did my creative funding idea just happen to pan out? As the lots sold for more than I expected, I was again forced to ask the question: Why?

Probably there are circumstances in your life where you have seen God at work and you too were forced to ask why. Why does he care? In our case, I had to ask what he wanted me to do with the money he entrusted to me.

You could argue that God wasn't as responsible for my early career success as was simple hard work, creativity, focus, and the willingness to take risks. Possibly, but the fact remains that in each circumstance, when the odds seemed most stacked against me, I asked God for help in finding a way. I knew in those moments that without his help, I would not find the solutions I needed. As a result, as we overcame each hurdle, I had to face the reality that God was helping me. But why? Why did he hear and why did he answer?

Did he want us to get rich so that we could live comfortably? Did he want me to build my identity around being a young, aggressive real estate developer? Or was he testing me to see where I would put my life focus, while building my faith in him along the way? Over my next ten years in business, I continued to experience this same cycle of God's provision.

I'll bet that if you were to track back through your own story, you would find this same thread. How was God's hand at work in *your* first half?

I believe God intentionally entrusted me with certain skills and resources for a purpose, and that purpose was not just so that I could live a nicer lifestyle, own a larger home, drive a faster car, dress better, eat at nicer restaurants, and take more interesting vacations. As I read my Bible, it became clear on almost every page that God had more in mind for us than just money, material things, power, or fame. I came to realize that while my view of success felt exciting, God's view was far greater—and much more fulfilling.

I had to reevaluate life in view of God's definition of success and, in light of that, determine what significance would look like in my life.

After all, I wondered, what purpose could I find in a life of pursuing nothing but leisure? How fulfilling would it be to retire early and spend the rest of my life just picking up shells on a beach somewhere? Wouldn't it get old after a few months or years of golfing five times a week or, as Billy Crystal says in the movie *City Slickers*, to drive an RV around the country in an endless pursuit of "the ultimate soft yogurt"?

I once planned a six-week vacation. The idea seemed idyllic. We would drive through the beautiful countryside of the eastern seaboard, spend a week in New Orleans exploring low country food and culture, bop back up to visit my family in central Pennsylvania (mostly to drop off our son, a baby at the time), fly to Miami and rent a boat with friends and sail to the

Bahamas and back, yada, yada, yada. On and on for six full weeks!

We began our dream vacation, but after three weeks of nothing but pleasing ourselves, the task of deciding what we wanted to do next became tedious. I found each day less and less enjoyable and felt a growing sense that just pleasing myself was meaningless. Believe it or not, we quit after four weeks. I couldn't wait to get back to real life. We simply couldn't take floating around for six weeks with no purpose other than our own pleasure.

Now, imagine being sentenced to spend the rest of your life like that, with nothing to show at the end, with no real value when the dust settled.

As a real estate developer, I understand the basics of property valuation. Buildings are valued based on their net income stream, projected over time. I found myself faced with the ultimate valuation task: to determine the highest and best use of my time, talent, and treasure, projected over time—or eternity.

Bottom line, I had to answer the question, Would I be a good steward of my time, talent, and treasure if I spent the rest of my life developing real estate? That turned out to be a more difficult question to answer than I expected, because none of the pat answers I had heard on either side of the equation really stood up to scrutiny. It's not always true that serving in full-time ministry is God's higher, more significant calling. Nor is it always true that God calls effective business people to a lifelong commitment of being salt and light in the "real world." This is a question you will have to answer for yourself in your own career and life circumstances.

Pause for a minute and reflect on a short verse from the Bible: "For we are God's workmanship, created in Christ Jesus to do good works, which God prepared in advance for us to do" (Ephesians 2:10).

As I reflect on this verse, I find it hard to grasp that the God who created the universe has work lined up for me to do, specific assignments he prepared in advance. We have all the skills and resources we need to begin—but he waits to see if we will put our hand to the task. He is counting on me to trust him and pursue his plan and his assignments.

When you stop to think about it, this verse tells us that God has already sorted out the answer to my question, 'Would I be a good steward of my time, talent, and treasure if I spent the rest of my life developing real estate?' He has given it careful thought and has already assigned me work to do based on what he knows is best. Now it's up to me to discover what those works are.

Ultimately, my wife, Linda, and I asked the pivotal question of the Halftime experience: *What does God have for us to do that will outlast us? How can I hold what I have loosely enough that it can be transformed into something that can never be taken away?*

What assets do you manage that could be used for the blessing of others? Perhaps part of your time (even ten hours a week), your position of influence, your honed management skills?

So how does God define success? For example, what benchmarks did Jesus use as he moved from his first-half career as a carpenter into his second-half ministry assignment?

As I have observed people in the Bible whom God calls successful, I have noticed that he is not at all opposed to individuals becoming high-capacity achievers, attaining goals, becoming both wealthy and influential. Whether or not they achieve those things has nothing to do with why God calls them successful. Instead I find that they earned the success label because they focused on God and consistently obeyed him.

On one level, the Bible makes it clear that God considered it success when Joseph attained favor and influence. In Genesis we read, "The warden paid no attention to anything under Joseph's care, because the LORD was with Joseph and gave him success in whatever he did" (39:23). Joseph enjoyed success because he followed God's direction for his life.

In the book of Joshua, we find the underlying foundation for successful living, based on following God's instruction. Joshua told God's people, "Do not let this Book of the Law depart from your mouth; meditate on it day and night, so that you may be careful to do everything written in it. Then you will be prosperous and successful" (Joshua 1:8).

Looking at life through God's end of the telescope, the Bible does not assume that someone who has wealth, favor, or a position of influence is automatically successful. God looks at life from an eternal perspective, and he counsels those who have these resources to "do good, to be rich in good deeds, and to be generous and willing to share. In this way they will lay up treasure for themselves as a firm foundation for the coming age, so that they may take hold of the life that is truly life" (1 Timothy 6:18–19).

When measured from a global or historical perspective, even the most moderately successful North American must be considered overwhelmingly affluent and privileged. Much of the world lives on an income of only a handful of dollars a month. God has richly endowed middle-class America and he will hold us accountable for how we use those resources.

The Bible gives a clear definition of what it considers a successful life. God may have enabled you to attain many of your first-half goals and allowed you to acquire many material things—yet he knows that those things will never satisfy your soul or provide long-term value. His true blessing is not found there.

The Bible challenges us to redefine success in higher terms than wealth, favor, and eminence. We are to pursue God's favor and his eternal reward by using our time, talent, and treasure in as leveraged a way as possible to become rich in good deeds. By doing this, God counsels us that we will make the ultimate investment, one that will reap eternal dividends.

Successful living means doing life in community with God, using what he has given us, at his direction and thereby laying up treasure in heaven. At the same time, he promises we will experience the adventure of what it means to really live.

That's what I want my life to be all about. To use what God has entrusted to me in the most leveraged way to accomplish tangible things and to enjoy the adventure of faith, doing life with him along the way.

Chapter 3

Like Punting into the Wind

There is a vast difference between wanting a life of more significance and actually pursuing it. As I described in chapter one, it took more courage than I expected to get past the romantic notion of "Wouldn't it be nice if my life had more meaning?"—with all the noble feelings that go with it—to actually drawing the line in the sand, intentionally redefining success, and pursuing significance.

It dawned on me, however, that I was trying to swim upstream. Or perhaps a better metaphor would be walking up a down escalator. In our Halftime language, it was like punting the football directly into a fiercely gusting wind—with all the uncertainties of where the wind might take the ball. Our culture is just such a strong wind, shouting at us what values it considers worthwhile, values that we all too easily allow to become our own internal motivators—money, fame, and power.

I wouldn't have thought those motivators had much pull on my heart, at least not the fame and power. But in Matthew 4, we find that Satan used these three temptations to try to entice Jesus to abandon God's plan for the last part of his life. If those were significant temptations for him, it makes sense that we ought to explore them as motivators that could stand in our way of redefining success and pursuing significance.

After all, once you decide to pursue significance, who knows where it could lead? You could end up giving ten hours a week in prison ministry, scaling back your fifty-hour week at the office to forty. As a result, you might not get the VP role in that new division. You could end up as a missionary in Africa or Macedonia.

God won't call most of us to Africa or Macedonia, but who can say what God has in mind for you? Once the ball leaves your foot, there is no telling where the wind might take it. Will it sail far downfield, or will the wind take it off to one side and out of bounds? Once you begin to turn your sights toward significance, there is no telling what the implications may be.

What are the "out-of-bounds" that we fear, and what can we do about them? There are at least five risks that many of us encounter. The good news is that the Halftime journey is all about turning the game plan over to God, who controls even the wind.

The Wind of Career Risk

Mike Shields is now a close friend and ministry partner, but when he first called, he was a total stranger. He called to ask if we could have dinner when he arrived in town on business. He felt he was in Halftime and wanted to chat about the experience. Since I had been through it and had helped others to move through this stage of life, he thought I might be able to help him think through the obstacles he faced. Little did he know how much I considered it a privilege to share the Halftime journey with talented, open-hearted individuals who really seek what God has in mind for them.

Mike worked at an investment management company on Wall Street. He was at the top of his game. He and his wife, Marion, had three beautiful children and lived in Greenwich, Connecticut. He loved the everyday adrenaline rush of making multimillion-dollar investment decisions; but his heart longed to invest his life in something bigger than a double-digit return on his clients' investment portfolios. And Marion wished he could be available to invest more significantly in their children's lives. Mike was successful but not ready to abandon his career, and as a high-energy, high-capacity leader, he would probably wither emotionally and intellectually if he simply quit his job to spend all his time focusing on family and ministry.

So every day Mike took the early train downtown, came home tired after the kids had gone to bed, and shared a late meal with his wife as they talked over family issues. Days blended into weeks, and his life zipped past while he wondered if he was doing what God had created him to do.

Mike needed to find a way to create some open space in his life, some way to live more and to discover a serving opportunity that would infuse significance into his days. To begin, he would have to renegotiate with his firm and find a win-win strategy that would permit him to cut his workweek to forty-five or fifty hours and travel less. But he feared that the moment he breathed a word of such a desire, either his boss or his peers might not respond positively—maybe very badly. They likely wouldn't understand his feelings that something seemed missing from his life; after all, from their perspective, he had the perfect job, home, and family. They might question his commitment to the team, which might well change the course of his career if he chose to stay in investment management. There was no telling what might happen when he punted the ball into the wind.

Ultimately Mike took the risk. He spoke openly with his boss about his desire to redefine success and create space for other things that he considered significant. His boss's reaction surprised Mike, and we'll talk about it later in this book. For you, however, punting into the wind is still an unknown risk.

Below the surface of this perceived career risk lies one of the most compelling human motivators: money.

The Wind of Financial Risk

Jesus talked more about money than almost any other single topic—because it's such a strong human motivator. He told us plainly that our hearts will focus wherever we put our money. When we redefine success in terms other than money, we open ourselves to the potential of having less money than we have now. Linda and I ventured into this dilemma with both eyes open—or at least, we thought so.

My guess is that if you are reading this book, you've already given careful thought to your priorities relative to money. It's a powerful tool that we can use to affect eternity. At the same time, the pursuit of money can limit how and whether God uses us. I never thought money had a strong hold on my heart, but I never carefully considered the subtleties of its power on me.

What I did not realize when we first began to cut back our earning potential to pursue serving opportunities is that I used money as a measuring stick to gauge my effectiveness. I used it more to rate my performance relative to that of my peers than to obtain security, comfort, or things.

Today money still exerts a certain power over me—especially now that my peers are at the peak of their earning years. To be honest, the fact that for the past ten years I have chosen to earn less money carries the risk that I no longer feel as though I measure up to some of my peers. Sometimes I feel I'm losing ground as I see their net worth escalate while mine stays flat-lined.

Money may exert more of a pull on your heart in the area of security or lifestyle. My wife, Linda, felt most concerned about the financial insecurities that came with redefining success. She wondered how our decision would impact what activities our children could participate in, how often she could travel back home to visit her family, and what would happen if we encountered a major, unanticipated expense.

From time to time, friends plan an expensive trip and ask us to join them; we may have to say no because it simply doesn't fit in the budget. Sometimes my close friends insist on treating me to something extravagant that they think I will enjoy, just because they know the sacrifice we have made. I am learning how to accept their generosity as a loving gift. It's not as easy as it sounds.

Choosing to pursue God's calling on your life is going to entail financial risk. Whether you are called to earn less by giving your time in service to others or to earn even more and thus become an open and clear channel for God's money to flow through you to others—either way, God will call you and I to choose where our ultimate allegiance lies.

Our faith and our finances are always connected. If you plan to punt into the wind of financial risk, you must carefully consider what sway money has on your heart and then intentionally offer it to God as a risk you are prepared to take.

Remember, God is not opposed to your being rich. He is, however, opposed to our pursuing money either as an attempt to become self-sufficient or to find the fulfillment that he knows can come only from living the life he means us to live.

The Wind of Opinion

I found myself kicking into the wind of opinion and common sense, which came, surprisingly, from well-meaning friends and family. Though they love me and want my best, they sometimes had radically different perspectives on what real success looks like.

They wondered why, if God was blessing my business, I would turn my attention away from it. What about my responsibilities to provide for my family? Wasn't it a little extreme to downsize our home and cut our family budget just so I could volunteer some time with a mission organization? After all, others (who don't have the same earning potential) can do that work full time. Wouldn't it be better if I just focused on making money in real estate and then wrote a check to the organization? I soon felt as though I were part of a weird fringe of over-zealous Christianity.

Think about this risk—your friends and business colleagues may view you as somewhat unbalanced or fanatical. It's one thing to have a firm idea of what we believe about God and the hereafter; it's quite another to go out on a limb and cut back on our career potential just for some pious idea.

I remember looking in the Bible and seeing stories of people like Daniel and Paul who totally sold out to God. I wondered why some around me looked at me as if I were losing my marbles. I aspired to be like Daniel and Paul. I wanted to finish well like Caleb.

The good news is that this wind of opinion forced me to begin to find my identity in God's view of my life, not in the opinion of others, and that is a journey I am still on.

The Wind of Being Ordinary

Although I am seldom tempted by fame—which sounds so egocentric, after all—still, something in my DNA finds it unacceptable to be "ordinary." The way we typically define success makes it necessary to stand above the crowd and, as a result, be rewarded and acknowledged. The thought of redefining success makes us wonder if we will simply give in to mediocrity.

While on a speaking trip in Russia last year, I heard two common expressions from those who had lived through communism—both are relics of the Soviet era: "The nail that sticks up gets pounded down" and "Initiative is punishable." *How completely un-American*, I thought. It opposes everything that has been driving me in my first half.

A recent TV ad for a career placement website pokes fun at this very issue. It shows interviews with preteen children describing their dreams for their grown-up years. Instead of dreaming of careers as firemen, architects, and nurses like we all did, these children say they dream of becoming what many of us have become at midlife. One boy says he dreams of growing up to be a "middle manager." A little girl suggests that she wants to be underappreciated and overworked; someone else dreams of growing up and having a big mortgage; another of being "a yes man."

How many of us had such low aspirations when we were young?

Few people who enjoy success in the first half of their lives aspire to be ordinary. They fear that if they change careers to pursue something more significant, or even if they take on a serving project alongside of their career, they will run the risk that they may not be as good at the next thing. I remember thinking, *I know how to do this real estate gig; but who's to say*

I won't fall flat on my face when it comes to helping a nonprofit organization or my church?

We have no intention of being "middle managers." We want to achieve something spectacular. In our most honest moments, we think something like this: *If I stick at my present career, I will someday be a big fish in this pond. Maybe even nationally recognized. But if I transition my focus toward serving others in some ministry, who's to say it will ever amount to much? After all, there is a chance I will be called by God to serve in some unrecognized role where no one ever knows how much I sacrifice or how much I gave up to be a blessing to others.*

Okay; good point. I've been there, and when I find myself there, I return to Matthew 6, where Jesus says, "Be especially careful when you are trying to be good so that you don't make a performance out of it. It might be good theater, but the God who made you won't be applauding" (*The Message*).

And if that is not clear enough, Jesus adds another caution:

> When you do something for someone else, don't call attention to yourself. You've seen them in action, I'sm sure—'play actors' I call them—treating prayer meeting and street corner alike as a stage, acting compassionate as long as someone is watching, playing to the crowds. They get applause, true, but that's all they get. When you help someone out, don't think about how it looks. Just do it—quietly and unobtrusively. That is the way our God, who conceived you in love, working behind the scenes, helps you out.

We may end up investing countless hours in the lives of poor inner-city children, and yet a high percentage of them may still end up in crime and poverty. You may be called to serve in a support role in church, unrecognized and unknown. You may be called to spend hours at home, working with your handicapped child while your spouse pursues her career—and only a handful of people will ever know your sacrifice. This is the wind that chilled me the most. This is the risk that I still struggle with today.

When we punt the ball, we give God a choice: Will he choose for us to serve him quietly in what seems like an ordinary role—without fame or glory? Or will he choose to use us in a big way, like Billy Graham? As I redefine success, ultimately I have to come to grips with whose acclaim I want. Am I satisfied with an audience of just one—God?

Halftime is not just having a midlife renaissance or a personal renewal. That might lead to a richer, deeper, more textured way of doing life than the two-dimensional focus on success that defines many of our first-half lives. But it will not enable you to find significance, because it is centered in self-absorption. Significance comes only as we give ourselves away—and giving your self away entails a cost.

More than twenty-five years ago, Elisabeth Elliot wrote in her book *These Strange Ashes* of leaving this country to serve a small tribe in remote South America. After working hard for nine months to understand their language, doing much of the groundwork that would become the foundation for translating the Bible into their language, all of her files, notes, and charts were stolen. Her only copy of nine months of hard work had vanished.

As her heart broke, she wondered why God would allow such a waste of time. In her words,

> Everything I had done in nine months in San Miguel de los Colorados was undone at a stroke. But no. It couldn't be. We would get it all back somehow. Lord, let it not be. . . . The tenth psalm came to mind: 'Why do you hide yourself in times of trouble?' And as before, I heard no reply to that and other questions. There was no light, no echo, no possible explanation. All the questions as to the validity of my calling, or, much more fundamentally, God's interest in the Colorado (people's) salvation, in any missionary work—Bible translation or any other kind—all these questions

came again to the fore. To be a follower of the Crucified means, sooner or later, a personal encounter with the Cross. And the Cross always entails loss. The great symbol of Christianity means sacrifice, and no one who calls himself a Christian can evade this stark fact.[1]

Her honesty has been a point of reference for me as I have faced this same fear.

If your second half is going to be significant, it is going to involve giving yourself away. Part of that sacrifice may come because you reoriented your time and talent in midlife toward serving others, a decision that short-circuited what you could have become in this world.

But just remember this: no one who sacrifices for God is "an ordinary person."

The Wind of Influence

A desire for power has never motivated me. But when I chose to redefine success and pursue significance, I found myself wondering if I would still be influential. As I pondered spending less time developing real estate and more time investing in the lives of others, I wondered if I would end up sidelined into some insignificant corner with little or no real influence on the real world. To leave a mark on our world, don't you have to rise to a position of power or prestige?

Frankly, I want to change the world. I want my life to count. I remember wondering, *If I choose not to become the biggest and most successful real estate developer possible, will I still have the kind of influence I need to change the world?* And I remember joking about the golden rule: "He who has the gold, makes the rules." I couldn't help but wonder, *Should I focus on making money because it brings a certain amount of influence?*

I remember thinking of so many mediocre Christian businessmen I knew who wore cheap, out-of-style clothes, drove gray four-door sedans, paid their mortgage faithfully, and seemed like nice guys—but from my perspective had almost no influence on their world. I have no desire to be just "a nice guy." I want to aggressively use every ounce of talent and energy God has given me to change the world. So a deep down question tugged at me: Do I have to become successful before I have that kind of influence?

Perhaps your present job provides a platform that enables you to influence the direction of your company, the future of many staff, the kids in your classroom, significant elements of your community, or even your entire industry. More likely, you can see that if you stay focused on your career, you will soon be in such a position of influence.

When you punt your time, talent, and treasure into the air and let God take it wherever he wishes, you fear losing the influence you long to have over your world.

A friend of mine runs the emergency medical services for a major US city. Joe is in his forties, has done this job for more than ten years, and is good at it. Every year his organization provides ambulance service to thousands of people around the city. During his tenure, his employees have shortened their response time to emergency calls and still have kept expenses below comparable costs of other cities. By any ordinary measure, Joe is successful. But he has sensed God's tug on his heart to do something more with his life—not to leave his job, not to be any less committed to serve the sick and injured in his city—but to invest some of his time and talent into an area he feels passionate about.

Joe has a platform to influence EMS in his city, but he feels called to create space in his life to invest in other ways. Suppose he took a less responsible role within the EMS, one that enabled him to have more flexible hours and perhaps not be on call all hours of the day and night, a move that would allow him to pursue other areas of service in his community. Would he still be able to make an impact without the CEO platform of influence? Can he creatively redesign his job to retain the CEO role and have time to allocate elsewhere?

As you reflect on this fear, remember how God moved Moses out of his position of power and influence in Egypt so that he could use him in an even more significant way. What Moses did in his first half was hardly insignificant; but it turned out to be only the foundation on which he built his second half.

Sometimes God calls us to invest ourselves in passing the baton to emerging leaders, to invest in the lives of younger men and women. The key is discovering what God has in mind for you and letting him provide the platform for influence.

The Wind of Doubt

Finally, I found myself kicking into the wind of doubt. That is, I pondered God's trustworthiness. Once I decided to step out of my comfort zone, outside the well-worn path of how I knew to "do" life and manage my world, I realized that I would have to *really* trust God. And frankly, I worried that he might not come through.

As a goal-oriented person, I tend to measure each day, month, and year based on what I accomplish. It was very easy in real estate to know what I had accomplished at the end of a month or year. It all boiled down to a bottom line. By contrast, investing our time and money in serving others often provides no clear, measurable outcomes.

If you have spent the past ten or twenty years at home raising a family, you have been able to track clearly the growth of your children, their measurable performance in school, sports, graduations, jobs.

After my first year of serving in the nonprofit realm my doubts grew because I had no way of knowing whether my investment in others had accomplished anything significant. Had the programs I helped to develop produced real results? When I failed to find the same kind of measurements that I knew in business, I faced the wind of doubt.

My financial plan had always assumed that I would make more money through my forties and fifties than I could if I were to reallocate time to serving opportunities. As I recalculated income and net worth projections, I could see that this journey would call on us to cut our family's expenses and to rely on God, so that no major financial setbacks would put us into a tailspin. And I just was not sure I could count on God like that. After all, the Bible talks about the diligent accumulating money little by little. Proverbs 10:4 says, "Lazy hands make a man poor, but diligent hands bring wealth." That's how I had accumulated our assets to that point; but now I had chosen intentionally not to focus on maximum earning.

Those are just two areas where I faced the wind of doubt. I had built my faith on the belief that God was there, that he loved me and wanted the best for me—but this step would require me to *really* rely on God. It felt like someone who knows that a chair is made to sit in, knowing that it is sturdy, but then refuses to sit down on it for fear that it might collapse. Or like the engineer who designed a short tunnel near Asheville, North Carolina, but who never actually dared to drive through it once it was built.

Seems to me that belief is only belief when we act on it. I found the wind of doubt-in-God blowing directly into my face as I considered kicking off my transition from success to significance.

What if I gave up the next real estate project to work on a project for a ministry, and then they didn't make good use of my time? What if I discovered that my skills in business did not transfer effectively into this new arena? What if, while I am working on this ministry stuff, I miss out on a really big deal—the deal of the decade?

Each of the five areas of risk is significant. Yes, it's possible that you could redefine success and reallocate your time and treasure only to find that

- your career suffers
- you are forced to make financial sacrifices

- your friends and peers do not understand you and don't seem to be behind you
- your influence diminishes
- at times you feel as though God has not held up his side of the bargain

Although you may not have thought of them before now, chances are that you would have before long. Knowing that they are likely to arise and that it's okay to talk about them is a major step to being able to deal with them in a healthy way.

I've experienced all five of these. But make no mistake—refusing to punt the ball in the first place is not a risk-free option. It has its own set of risks. In football, if you are unwilling to punt the ball, you run the risk of turning the ball over to your opponent near your own end zone. And that is not a winning strategy.

You and I face significant risks either way. I can choose to live the second half of my life confined to what I think is safe, without exploring and pursuing what I was created to do—and risk missing out on the incredible opportunity of partnering with God in what he is doing in this world. Or I can take a deep breath, kick the ball with all my might, and launch into the greatest adventure of life.

If you are like Bill Beattie, you are wondering if doing nothing about God's promptings is the safer approach. Doing nothing about Halftime may not be as safe an alternative as you may think.

Not only do you risk squandering the talents you were given on things that won't matter in one hundred years, but you also might risk getting eaten by an alligator. If you're not buying it, ask Bill.

"Basically," he says, "it's a story of my ignoring a gentle nudge from God but then finally responding to his less subtle revelation on the Zambezi River to 'do my work in the Danbury, Connecticut, inner city, *now!*'"

Bill says his wife, Kathie, and he were comfortable and generally pleased with their life in Danbury. Their three children were leading productive lives, his business was doing well, and they were about to celebrate their thirty-fifth wedding anniversary. He had recently been elected to the board of elders of his local church and, at age fifty-eight, he envisioned an opportunity to serve the needs of his congregation as an elder—a wise, seasoned counselor.

"Kathie and I decided to return to Africa for our anniversary celebration, since we had spent six great years there in the seventies when I was regional director for Union Carbide," Bill says. "Before embarking on our anniversary celebration trip, a good friend since football days at Lehigh University, John Stanley, sent me the book *Halftime*. I consumed the short book in two and a half hours and was impacted by Bob Buford's challenge for Christians to pause, plan, and commit the second half of their lives to the Kingdom of God, using God's gifts and the experiences of their first half. I thanked John for the book but concluded that in spite of God's nudging and my belief in the Halftime concept, any real action plan would have to be deferred until I had completed my elder board service and retired in three to four years.

"One of the highlights of our trip was a canoeing adventure on the Zambezi River near Mano Pools in the Zambezi River Valley. This is a beautifully wild part of Zimbabwe along the route that David Livingstone followed in the mid-nineteenth century. Today there are still hippos and napping fifteen-foot crocodiles throughout the length of the river. The major difference was that whereas Livingston was skilled in handling himself on the river, I was a novice canoeist and had foolishly rejected Kathie's suggestion of canoeing lessons prior to the trip.

"Once the training session was completed (five minutes in all), we left in our respective canoes. The plan was fairly obvious: canoe downstream, ensuring that the hippos were always provided a deep river route relative to the canoe. In other words, stay between the shore and the hippo. Although I had twenty years of experience in Africa and many safaris under my belt, as a former inner-city kid raised in Philadelphia with little river experience, I felt somewhat out of my element. Once we started canoeing down the river, eyeball to eyeball with hippos at every turn, I *knew* I was out of my element. The fear in my wife's eyes whenever she turned to see if I saw the hippos directly in front of us, did not reassure me.

"We survived the morning and our guide advised us that the major challenge for the afternoon would be tree stumps submerged in the river. 'Avoid them or risk capsizing the canoe,' was his insightful suggestion.

"Of course, we hit a tree stump early in the afternoon while trying to avoid a threatening hippo downstream. The canoe did capsize and we held on to the canoe while the rescue canoe sped to us. Kathie was picked up, but there was no room in the canoe for a fourth person without risking all parties. As I attempted to right the canoe—or somehow climb on top of it—I knew one of the crocs might take a liking to me. Little did I know that a thirteen-foot crocodile came within ten feet of me before turning and pursuing some of the flotsam from the canoe that had gone floating down river.

"That evening at the campfire, as I reflected on our river experience and the extraordinary fact that the croc did not attack and drag me to the bottom, I sensed that God had intervened on my behalf to save me for his purposes. Although we joked among the team about the croc's discriminating choice of me or the sandwich bag, that night I felt God's presence and his calling me to service.

"The next morning, I told Kathie of my spiritual experience and that I would retain the stubby mustache that I had grown in the bush as an ongoing reminder of God's grace and mercy and my commitment to serve him. Each new day, in the mirror, I am reminded of what a great and merciful God we serve.

"When we returned to the US, I immediately sought where and how I could serve God in the context of the Halftime theme. I took time to assess my background, strengths, and passion for the underdog. Friends encouraged me to seek a role in the inner city, particularly with 'at risk' youth. I founded the Pathways Danbury Mentoring Ministry to reach out to 'at risk' boys in Danbury. Our ministry provides one-on-one mentoring by Christian men for boys in middle school through high school. The key to the ministry continues to be the sharing of Jesus by good men on a long-term basis to kids who are at risk for drugs and alcohol, poor school performance, delinquency, and family instability.

"In addition, we provide Bible study and tutoring during the school year, as well as summer Bible camp for all boys. Each boy who graduates from high school receives a $10,000 grant for his education, business, or housing needs. This year, the first Pathways young man graduated from high school and will attend college in September. Approximately twenty to twenty-five kids are in the program and are supported by approximately thirty-five men serving as mentors or on our steering committee.

"Looking back on my first-half experiences, there is no doubt that God was training me for work of the kingdom in the second half of my life. I recommend to all those reaching their 'Halftime break' to follow the Halftime process for planning the second half of their life. It is not only an exciting and satisfying human experience, but it is a means of doing God's work when you are best prepared and equipped to do it."

Bill advises you and me that if we feel too afraid to take the risk at Halftime and follow God's call on our lives, then, for goodness' sake, stay away from crocodiles.

You Are Not Alone

Redefining success and pursuing significance means swimming upstream. It means punting into the wind. But you are not alone!

Maybe that's the most surprising thing you will discover in your Halftime journey. Many times after I speak at a conference to a room full of middle-aged business and professional leaders, I ask participants to name the greatest value of the day. More often than not they say, "I looked around at a room full of peers who are wrestling with the same issues, and I discovered I'm not alone. I'm not going crazy after all."

So what will this new journey look like? And how do you find freedom to pursue what God is calling you to? Let's consider those questions next.

Chapter 4

Halftime as Seen
from the Goodyear Blimp

alftime is a journey—a process—not an event or a decision. Ultimately, this journey is more about what we are becoming than what we are doing or accomplishing. God will likely use your Halftime journey as part of the preparation for how he wants to use you in your second half. Many people, including myself, have found that difficulties in midlife transition are important opportunities God uses to shape us so that he can use us more effectively.

If you could observe a number of Halftime journeys from the Goodyear blimp, ten thousand feet above the playing field, what would you see? Would there be a common path they follow? And what could you learn from those who have gone before?

The Halftime journey that most of us take is somewhat fluid but has distinct stages. Gaining an overview of those stages can help you put the chaos of your feelings into a context that is, frankly, normal for many of us.

I have lunch almost every week with someone who is in Halftime. They begin by describing their feelings and, as a result, what they are considering doing. Invariably they describe the same journey that thousands already have taken; but they almost always feel as though they are the first to have such an experience.

I listen carefully as they describe their career path after college, the extreme focus on work, and the commitment that has led to their success. Then they describe how it began to dawn on them that they may have missed something along the way. I often chuckle as they search for words to describe what is missing now in their lives: "I want my second half of life to have more ... um ... I guess the word is ... significance."

How freeing it would be for them if they only knew that they were at the beginning stage and had a clear map of the road ahead!

Several months ago an executive called to ask if I would go to lunch with him to discuss the direction of his life. As Jim and I talked, it struck me how typical he is of most people who are approaching Halftime. He described graduating from business school, and with some friends presenting a creative idea to one of the major banks to enter a new market. The bank funded the new partnership, and Jim and his team spent the next twenty years on the ride of their lives.

When Jim first called me, he was not sure what was wrong, but he knew he had to make some changes. He has a wonderful wife and two beautiful kids, but he's seldom around. As he said, "I am one of the top four hundred frequent flyers for US Air, which I consider an indictment." He wondered how he could begin to balance his life and discover his personal passions without giving up what he loves to do and has built into a great enterprise. He had no idea that others had taken this journey or that a road map could show him how to have a healthy transition.

I asked Jim a few probing questions to try to discover where his journey had led him. I asked him what he felt was missing from his life, what he loved about his work, what he was a "ten" at (in other words, what he was really great at, as opposed to merely competent). We both soon realized that it would serve him well if he could methodically work through a self-assessment process and develop a personal mission statement. It is so hard to identify our personal passions when all we have ever done is our work.

I asked Jim if he had any close friends who could walk with him through this journey. He looked off into the distance as he carefully scrolled down in his mind the list of his closest friends. He spoke out loud as he scanned down the mental list: "I'm really close with my wife; I have great neighbors; my partners and I have been through thick and thin together, even though we don't really connect beyond transactions; I know some of the guys at church—but to be honest with you, no. I really don't have any close friends."

At lunch I described the Halftime journey for him, pausing to answer his questions. And then I provided him with a list of the best next steps that he could take. When he left that day, Jim had a commitment from me to help him and a clear road map for his journey.

Today Jim has retooled his career, balanced his family time, and begun to pursue the areas of passion that will infuse a sense of eternal significance into his life. And he is also on a journey of cultivating the deep, intimate friendships he will need.

Regardless of where you are in your journey, this chapter will enable you to pinpoint your stage and anticipate what lies ahead. This road map would have been so valuable for me if someone had layed it out in this way.

After you review this map, subsequent chapters will provide you with next steps and stories that make the journey come alive.

Scan through this journey and determine where you are. What questions would you add to this list, specific to your life? Write them in.

Stage One: Discovering Vision

When you first discover that your second half can be marked by even more joy and impact than your first half you are in stage one of Halftime. Stories of how others have made the journey from success to significance expand your vision of the possibilities just ahead for you and you begin to dream. At the beginning of your Halftime experience, you, like Jim, probably won't even recognize that you've started a new era of your life. Many people at midlife who begin to sense something missing find it confusing and unsettling.

A significant life event may have triggered this unease, such as your youngest child leaving for college, the death of a parent, perhaps a divorce, or a significant success or failure in your career. For others, it is simply a calm stretch of water that presents a small opportunity to look around and see where life has taken them. We want to celebrate our success, recognizing that it is the foundation for our second half—but something nagging inside says that it has not delivered what we expected.

Regardless of the door through which you enter Halftime, a handful of questions pop up at the earliest moments:

- I have achieved some real success in my first half of life; in fact, I have accomplished much of what I set out to do. But is there more to life than my current situation?
- What do I consider eternally significant?
- What on earth would give my life meaning? What is my real purpose on earth?
- Am I alone in feeling this way?
- How much (stuff, money, advancement) is enough?
- Was my first half experience a foundation for something more significant in my second half?

Write in your other questions here:

- _____
  _____
- _____
  _____
- _____
  _____
- _____
  _____
- _____
  _____

Stage Two: Guided Reflection

At stage two of your Halftime journey you will sense the need for a systematic way to reflect on your past, on your passions and skills, reflect on God's Word, and start to see possi-

bilities for a life of impact and adventure take shape. You may begin to wonder if God has created you in a specific way for a unique purpose on this earth. As you explore who God has made you to be, you may be asking yourself some of the following questions:

- What am I really passionate about? What makes me come alive?
- What are my greatest strengths and core values?
- How can I make it work with my financial situation?
- What is my calling in life? What will be my personal mission statement?
- What role do I play most effectively in an organization?
- What is my spouse thinking about her/his second half and what is our vision together?
- Who can come alongside me in this journey and provide wisdom and insights? Who can help me make sense out of this time of life?

Write your other questions here:

- _____
  _____
- _____
  _____
- _____
  _____
- _____
  _____

Stage Three: Diverse Exposure

The third stage of Halftime is about intentionally looking outward to explore what God's already doing in the world and start to look for alignment with what you are excited about doing with your time, talent, and treasure. Through this exposure you will continue to gain more clarity about your unique calling.

Where the Guided Reflection stage is about introspection, the Diverse Exposure stage is about Exploration. Through low cost probes, you test drive serving opportunities and debrief those experiences with your spouse and a few close friends.

The stage of Diverse Exposure also involves preparing yourself and those around you for your new view of the world. It's about preparing your finances, researching and testing service opportunities, setting expectations with those with whom you "do" life, and getting the training you need for this journey. Consider a few appropriate questions at this stage:

- In what arena should I serve: the marketplace, my church, my community, or in some very needy area of the world?
- How do I begin to find service opportunities that fit me?
- What unique configuration of family, work, recreation and service best fits what I feel called to do?
- What elements of my life do I need to renegotiate to enable me to pursue significance?
- Should I stay engaged in my business with new parameters on my time and a renewed sense of purpose?
- How can I begin to create the margin in life to explore all that I feel called to do?
- How do I prepare my family and myself for this transition?
- What are my spouse's biggest dreams for this next season and how can I get behind them?
- What responsibilities do I have to my parents, and how will that affect what I can do in my second half?
- What legacy will I leave through my children and grandchildren?

Write in your other questions here:

- _____
- _____

- _____
- _____
- _____

Stage Four: Enduring Impact

In the last leg of your Halftime journey you engage fully with what you are called to do and be in your second half; you find a new equilibrium in life. It's about finding the right balance of serving, mixed in with your career, family, and recreational pursuits that will make it sustainable.

Many find that, after a while, the grass that seemed greener on the other side of the fence turns into hard work. It is all too easy to go back to what you feel comfortable with vocationally. As one person admitted, "My first-half career was at a point where I could fly the course blindfolded." All the hard work you did in the Diverse Exposure stage, testing out serving opportunities and making sure of your new calling in life, will pay dividends now.

Normally this phase includes time adjusting to the culture of the non-profit world, if that is where you land, learning new skills and assessing if you have found the right fit. You may ask yourself:

- How do I decide between the serving opportunities I have experimented with?
- What is the optimal blend of ministry: local/national/international; life-on-life/organization leadership?
- How can I integrate into this new ministry without losing what has made me successful?
- What is my highest and best contribution? How will I measure my contribution?
- Am I growing closer to God and to those I love as I pursue a second half of eternal significance?

Write in your other questions here:

- _____
  _____
- _____
  _____
  _____
- _____
  _____
- _____
  _____
- _____
  _____

Tom Hill lived out this journey. This successful financial advisor with Merrill Lynch paused to reflect on life, explored options for his second half, and negotiated a creative, unique life plan that fits him, his employer, and his family to a tee. Tom's story will enable you to see this journey played out in real life.

Tom is the kind of guy who doesn't mind if his mashed potatoes mingle with his peas. He is not a compartmentalized guy. "Ministry is life and life is ministry," says Hill. "I see all of it as one."

So it's okay if his four daughters tag along while he's working to help a church in rural Arkansas or if his wife sits in on one of his meetings with men transitioning to significance.

Hill, now forty-nine, grasped this Halftime concept early on.

"When I was at Vanderbilt, my main desire was to pursue God," he says, "so I began my career with a clear understanding that I had to pursue a successful career and be involved in ministry at the same time. I came to Merrill Lynch in 1981 with a deep desire to learn and succeed, but I also came with a prayer: 'God, I want to do this, but only if I can do this in a way that's pleasing to you. I don't want to compartmentalize ministry and marketplace.'"

Hill kept that focus throughout his twenties and thirties, developing his career as a broker, while he embraced ministry opportunities—from leading singles, seniors, young kids, and small groups to planting churches. In his forties he began to zone in on what he was most passionate about and what his real talents were. He was able to try a variety of ministries and test the waters freely. He views his church, Fellowship Bible Church Little Rock (*www.fbclr.org*), as the incubator for his God-given gifts.

In January of 2000, Hill sensed a call to refocus his efforts on serving other men at midlife, but without leaving Merrill Lynch.

"Threads in my life were coming together in a unique way. Thanks to God's provision, I had some financial flexibility. And my church was beginning to build bridges to the community, bridges that I wanted to help construct. It was time to step to the edge of adventure. I spent six months in prayer and discussions with my wife and other godly people; and in July of 2000, I approached my partners at Merrill Lynch about a part-time arrangement. They were surprised but supportive."

Hill still works most of the week at Merrill Lynch, but has carved out some extra time to pour into ministry and family pursuits. His primary ministry is through his church, helping other men in midlife transition.

"Several years ago, I realized that my church wasn't really ready for the wave of people Peter Drucker describes as 'having longevity and affluence—those able to manage themselves.' I wanted to be able to help my church prepare for that."

If you sat down with Tom to walk back through his Halftime journey, you would find that he was a pretty normal Christian guy. At some point, however, God called him to take significant risk and step out of a normal career path to allocate part of his time and talent away from career advancement. He discovered what he is good at and what he is passionate about and then went looking for a serving opportunity that would fit with Merrill Lynch, mesh with his wife's needs, and make a leveraged impact on this world.

Tom uses his role in the marketplace as a platform from which to speak into the lives of other men. He's having the time of his life. Tom's journey was made easier by many of the resources you'll find drawn together in the coming chapters.

And the first issue is discovering your greatest passion.

As you have reflected on the normal Halftime journey and what it looks like from the Goodyear Blimp, thousands of feet above the playing field—where are you in that journey? Throughout the rest of this book we are going to walk through the critical issues at each stage of the journey. Chances are, if you are well down the road, you will find ideas and steps that you missed along the way. Don't be afraid to circle back and give those areas some thought! Halftime is not always a linear process.

Chapter 5

Finding Your Wellspring of Success

Many people arrive at midlife with their passion and talent smoldering under layers of wet blankets. Those God-designed desires and core motivators have been covered up by responsibility, the pressure of keeping the plates spinning, and a sense that there simply is no possibility of pursuing what makes your heart beat fastest.

Strange as it may sound, my passion for real estate emerged at age fourteen. It was just a short drive from Philadelphia to the Jersey Shore for summer vacation. Often on the drive home, my dad would talk about how the price of property near the ocean was going up fast. I would sit in the back seat, mulling over how someone could buy land while it was still affordable.

While that may be an odd thought process for a fourteen year old, nevertheless I begged Dad to help me purchase a piece of tick-infested, overgrown land near the ocean that I thought would make a wise investment. It seemed to me that, since they are not making any more beach these days, that land would always be in demand.

I will never forget the thrill of walking out onto those five acres for the very first time. I could already envision what this place could look like someday with a beautiful summer home on it. I had a passion to create, and this land seemed like a blank canvas. Something deep inside my soul ignited that day, something so much a part of who I am that I was almost power-less to avoid its pull. I spent hours at night dreaming in bed of what I could do with the land. What I could not envision during those teenage years, however, was how my emerging passion and talents in real estate would impact my entire life.

I was never an outstanding student, but I had been given something that proved far more important than SAT scores. I had an innate drive and passion to create, combined with laser-sharp focus. Throughout high school and college I had a deep desire to put every penny I could earn toward the next land purchase.

It never dawned on me until later that God had provided the talents, the passion, the focus, and even the circumstances that enabled me to begin to use my talents early in life, for a purpose. Those same traits led to a measure of first-half success in real estate development. But as my business grew, Linda and I paused to reflect on God's purpose behind all of it. I felt in a continual rush. A rush to get on with the next thing without understanding that this first-half success formed an important step in the process God was using to prepare me.

Later I would look back on these formative years and see a strange combination of the eternal and the temporal. Now twenty years later, as I reflect back, I see God at work, shaping the abilities and passions he had given me and enhancing them in the marketplace, so that they could be used in my second half in even more significant ways.

If I were able to relive my first half, I would change my perspective about what God was doing. God is not in a rush and never will be. He uses our first half in a sanctified way for his own ends. Now, as I look back on my early business career, I see the beauty of normal marketplace skills being developed and used and honed by God. And today they form the well-spring of my second-half ministry.

Chances are that if you have achieved some measure of career success, a similar passion and gifting has surfaced. They may be in different areas altogether and may have surfaced later in life, but to you and those who work with you, they seem clear. Perhaps you sense, as I did, that they were hardwired into your DNA by the Creator of the universe.

If you really want to take an important first step toward transforming your experiences into eternal significance, you must come to the realization that you honor God by using your natural talents and drive in the area of your passion.

Yet remember—the passion that fires our success in the first half of life can also be the fire that destroys our health and our relationships. Fire can produce so much good, but it can also kill, char, and ruin if it is not controlled and confined.

When Jim Beckett, the forty-seven-year-old CEO of Beckett Publications, walked into the emergency room—chest aching, face ashen—the nurse asked him only one telling question: "Sir, what is your occupation?"

Jim's reply was his ticket to a cardiac crash room where, two short minutes later, and for five very long minutes, he was literally a dead man.

"It's hard to be driven when you're dead," says Jim. "So I've always thought the occupation question was intriguing."

Truth is, that nurse had probably seen many "Jims" walk through the emergency room door: *Type A. Driven. Hundred-hour workweeks etched on a gray face. The mighty entering on foot and leaving in a hearse.*

But God had something else in mind for Jim. He wanted to give Jim the opportunity to reach down deep into his passion for creative, strategic thinking and channel it in a different way. God wanted to get his complete attention so that he could help Jim use his drive and talent (the wellspring of success in his first half of life) and channel part of it toward something eternal—without selling his business or quitting his job.

"I define my life as before and after the heart attack," he explains. "A person in my situation is either going to run to the Savior or away from him. Because of the tough physical times surrounding my attack and a deep personal loss that sprang from it, I now have a new focus on serving."

Jim still loves his business. Still loves printing sports cards and anything connected to sports memorabilia. But now he carves out Thursday mornings each week to meet with a different ministry in his city of Dallas and help them discover and begin to fix the biggest challenge limiting their success.

Jim and his long-time friend, Joe Galindo, host a "quasi-brainstorming session" to bring together the leaders of the ministry they are targeting that week. The "working lunch" is called SHINE (Strategic consulting, Hospitality, Intercessory prayer, Networking and Encouragement). It's low on formality but full of positive interaction.

"Ministry guys have huge hearts and are wonderful to be around, but few go to business school—and many have business problems. They're open but not experienced."

That's where Jim's buddies come in.

"Most of my friends have typically been tapped only for their treasure. I'm trying to get them in the game by tapping their time and talents so they,re able to leverage them in some way. It creates a place between being a donor and being an actual 'partner,' like the book *Halftime* describes. It's a place where you're an interested, encouraging friend—and that's a good step toward forming a relationship."

Recently Jim invited some buddies with Internet savvy to lunch with a ministry that has a unique Bible translation it wants to bring to the Internet.

"We batted the concept around. My business friends were saying, 'Wow! No one has ever asked me how to bring something like that to market.' Of course, they'd done it with other stuff; so they shared their experiences. It was a lot of fun."

Jim loves using his networking abilities to bring marketplace leaders together with ministry leaders and enable them to enrich each others' lives and ministries.

"Many ministry leaders don't realize they share a commonality of experience and interest with marketplace guys. Marketplace guys often don't realize just how eager they are to share. My goal is to encourage these teams to get together in a temporary, no stress, no-strings-attached environment.

"SHINE is simply me expressing my gifts for the kingdom," says Jim. "And it's my way of encouraging others to do the same."

If you ask Jim to name the most exciting day of the week, he will tell you it's Thursday. Jim has redefined success and is pursuing significance, using the same passion and talent that made his first-half business successful.

Halftime for Jim is not about leaving his job or reinventing himself. Instead, what he has chosen to do is very much within reach of all of us. He simply carves out five hours a week to take the passion and talent he honed in the marketplace and uses it to serve a ministry with eternal impact. His first-half learning, skills, and passions enable him to have significant impact on his world in his second half of life.

While our hearts resonate with the idea of moving from success to significance, we sense that our first half was hardly insignificant. It served as a learning and proving ground. I cannot look back on my first half with any sense that it lacked significance. Rather, I see it as a training ground for what would prove to be more significant—the platform for my second half.

If Jim Beckett had not cultivated his ability in strategic thinking, if he had not built a trusted network of effective business leaders, he would not be able to make the unique contribution he is making today.

The essence of this important step is captured in a line from the movie *Chariots of Fire*, when the Olympic runner Eric Lidell says, "When I run, I sense God's pleasure." Lidell had realized that to live in the fullness of who God made him to be was to embrace the intersection of the secular with the divine. The Bible challenges us to "above all else guard your heart, for it is the wellspring of life" (Proverbs 4:23). God knows that the wellspring of what he wants to do through us in our second half comes from what he has placed in our hearts.

Just think of Moses' life. After forty years of marketplace success, Moses spent his midlife in the wilderness. At Halftime, Moses had to unlearn some things from the first half, perhaps detox some from his role and position in Egypt and allow God to form in him the kind of character that would ultimately allow him to make a significant eternal impact during the last years of his life.

If I were redoing my first half, I would ask God for the faith to use my talents and passions to their highest potential in the marketplace, believing that he was crafting a foundation to use me ultimately in a special place to influence more than just the material world. I would savor the joy of being able to partner with him as a close friend in those formative years.

More than that, I would begin earlier to define and refine the unique abilities and passions I have been given. These things form the wellspring of a significant second half of life.

What are your primary natural abilities? What are your passions? And how do they translate into a mission statement that can guide your life?

What makes you outstanding in some areas?

What things do you do now simply because you are competent at them? You have received good performance reviews over the years in that area, so you continue to operate as you always have. But in what other areas are you outstanding, areas that account for only a small percentage of your time and effort?

Jim Beckett has discovered that his greatest contribution and his greatest area of passion combine in the area of strategic thinking. He can contribute most to the ministries in Dallas by limiting his efforts to strategy and thought leadership. By doing this, Jim feels energized by the time each Thursday rolls around, knowing that his serving time is used in the most leveraged way.

How can you determine your greatest strengths and your greatest passions? The path to discovering our God-given passion differs for each of us. Some of us could benefit by doing a gifts and passion assessment survey. Such a tool provides a framework to reflect on our experiences and emotions surrounding those experiences. In coming chapters we will drill down deep into this area and help you to reach your serving goals through a self-assessment process.

You will also benefit from hearing stories from a wide variety of individuals who have discovered their passion and then reflecting on how you resonate or do not resonate with their interests. You can read dozens of stories of what others are doing in their second half of life at *www.halftime.org*.

For me, the process of discovering my area of passion and gifting involved a longer road of experimentation—beginning first with learning how to understand and connect with my feelings. Most of us discover our passion as we get moving on the road to significance and as we try new things and get involved with initiatives that capture our imagination. What changes, however, is that we now look for and feel more intentionally the experiences God brings across our path as we seek to discover our greatest passions.

For most of my first half of life, it did not matter how I *felt* about my work; what mattered was my effectiveness. While I happened to love the strategy and creativity of developing real estate, I had not searched for what made me passionate. At the end of every day and every project, I benchmarked myself not on how enjoyable the experience felt, but solely on my productivity. I did not understand that the two are inextricably connected. I had never given much thought to what the Bible said about God's intricate design of me—including my passions and abilities.

In Psalm 139 the psalmist says to God,

> *For you created my inmost being;*
> *   you knit me together in my mother's womb.*
> *I praise you because I am fearfully and wonderfully*
> *   made;*
> *   your works are wonderful,*
> *   I know that full well.*
> *My frame was not hidden from you*
> *   when I was made in the secret place.*
> *When I was woven together in the depths of the earth,*
> *   your eyes saw my unformed body.*
> *All the days ordained for me*
> *   were written in your book*
> *   before one of them came to be.*
> *How precious to me are your thoughts, O God!*
> *   How vast the sum of them (vv. 13–17).*

In these verses we learn that God designed you very intentionally and that in that design he took into account all the days and activities that he ordained for you. Seems to me that if he was intentional to put into me the skills and passions that he knew would be critical to the work he ordained for me, then I need to go the extra mile to discover and cultivate those skills and passions.

Rosalind Cook would agree. The first time she sank her hands into a mound of clay at the age of twenty-six, her soul said, "Ah-ha!"

"Shaping that clay into a meaningful form was like finding a piece of myself that had been missing for a long, long time," Cook declares. But life was busy, and for years Cook considered sculpting terra cotta clay merely a hobby. She had plenty to do as a teacher of the blind before becoming a stay-at-home mother of three, especially since she also served on a plethora of school boards and fund-raising committees.

"I realized I was trying to be who other people thought I should be, and I wasn't looking at how God created me," she says. "I pulled away from community work and reflected on what really gave me joy in life—and that was sculpting. But I still felt a bit guilty about loving it so much, until a missionary friend watched as I pulled out my clay one evening. I cried as I said to him, 'I don't understand how I can have so much joy in doing this! Where's the significance? This isn't saving souls. This isn't doing anything for anyone. It just feeds me and brings me joy.'

"That wise man of God replied, 'Rosalind, you are made in God's image. He's your Creator, and when you use the gifts of his image, that gives him pleasure.'

"From that day on, I gave myself permission to sculpt," says Cook. "And I finally connected with its true significance in my life. I was forty-one. I cast my first bronze at forty-two and was able to sell it almost immediately."

Today, Cook's prized bronze sculptures, which range from happy, playful children to full-sized images of Jesus, grace galleries throughout the world. She has donated many pieces to charities, raising far more money than any committee work she ever did.

"My art is a celebration of life and its Creator," says Cook. "It gives me the opportunity to motivate people to give themselves permission to dream. When I gave myself permission to take joy in clay, God sculpted a new world for me in the second half of life. If you delight in your God-given passion, he will give you the desires of your heart—because he put them there! Don't ignore what God is tugging at your heart to do; that's like saying what he has created for you isn't important. Pursue what gives you joy, and you will be amazed by the significance of what God will do through you."

As author Harry Kemp wrote somewhere, "The poor man is not he who is without a cent, but he who is without a dream."

What are the dreams and passions of your heart that, when combined with your abilities, could lead to the most exciting adventure of your life?

You may have just stopped short here and told yourself that you can't dream, not realistically, anyway. You have too many responsibilities and obligations to feel the freedom to dream. You are not financially in a place where you can just quit your job or sell your company and walk away to discover and pursue your dreams. Many of us at midlife feel this same pressure and confinement. It is, in part, what leads many people to a midlife crisis. Others settle for the boredom of a life lived outside of their destiny.

Instead you can have a constructive Halftime journey and live the second half of life in the sweet spot of what you were created to do. Any one of these three options remains open to you, even if you are not wealthy or even if you desire to stay with your present career.

As Oliver Wendell Holmes so eloquently said, "Most people go to their graves with their music still in them."

PART II

MOVING FROM DREAMS TO ACTION

Chapter 6

The Second Quarter: Pursuing Success with Significance in Mind

For most of us, the second quarter of life—our twenties and thirties—serves as a launching pad. After college we turn our attention to building a career. We enjoy the thrill of early wins, the promotions and good performance reviews, mixed in with periodic disappointments. Our all-consuming focus is our work. If we are married, we spend these years learning to adjust to each other. Little children often add to the challenge of just making life work. It's about creating our identity and building our career.

For me, the second quarter of life was a thrilling and captivating season. The casual observer might have considered my life a little out of balance. I worked six days a week, and in the evenings, once the kids were in bed, I worked long into the night. Developing real estate can be intense and fraught with unexpected regulatory hurdles, architectural design challenges, marketing hiccups, and endless wrangling with the bank—but it is intoxicating. I loved every minute of it (well, almost every minute).

But this focus was intentional. I had thought it through. Linda and I had spent time considering what we wanted for our lives. We had an end game in mind. I aimed to work very hard during those early years so that I would have some flexibility at midlife to allocate a portion of my time toward something bigger than me, something I was created to do. Having a plan enabled us to pursue success with significance in mind.

Because our goal called for me to use part of my time to serve others, in the midst of those most intense years we methodically began to reorient our lives to provide flexibility and margin so that we could begin to listen to God's direction and investigate ministry opportunities. Let me walk through some examples of how this played out in our lives so that you can begin to think about how something similar may play out in your life.

First, the goal affected the kind of real estate I developed. Because I wanted something that would produce a reliable income, I chose senior housing rather than single-family residential or commercial/industrial real estate. This strategy provided our family with stable growth in income and asset value over the medium to long term but did not produce significant cash up front. If we had been focused on owning a larger home and nicer cars, we might have chosen a different kind of real estate to develop.

I did not get involved in business opportunities that would take ten to fifteen years of intensive management, because I knew we wanted more flexible time within five to seven years.

When profits came in from one project, we did not let it ramp up our standard of living, because we knew that would be unsustainable in a few years if I had begun to dedicate a portion of my time to ministry.

Because my wife knew what I was trying to do in this intense work period, she felt comfortable with the long hours I gave to my career. She gave me the freedom to work really hard without feeling as if I were either being selfish or letting my family down. I had given her specific commitments regarding how long I would work with such intensity and how it would ultimately benefit our family.

There is freedom in knowing why you are investing your life in a certain way. Even within the most focused and intense second quarter of life, knowing that you are about more than career advancement and building your net worth gives you the freedom to chart a course that will position you well at midlife. So many of us default into jobs, mortgages, vacations, and lifestyles without knowing exactly why.

Charting a course for your second half without a plan and personal mission statement is like sailing on the ocean without a compass. I learned this lesson while sailing from Fort Lauderdale to the Bahamas with eight friends. Shortly after leaving the Florida coast, our radio directional finder stopped working, leaving us without an accurate frame of reference to pinpoint our location. We underestimated the currents of the Gulf Stream, and it consequently pushed us further north than we anticipated—too far north to see the islands that were supposed to prompt us to turn south to Nassau. Rather than sailing nine hours, ultimately we sailed for thirty-six hours before seeing land.

This extended time on the ocean, without a frame of reference, taught me two important life lessons. First, when you sail out of sight of land, it feels as though you are sailing straight ahead. Only when you begin to chart your course do you see all the zigging and zagging you've done. Second, as we worked to get the sails trimmed perfectly to move us as fast as possible, we all had a sick feeling in our stomachs that we just might be headed in the wrong direction altogether.

You may find that your second half of life begins with a renewed awareness of what you deem significant. That new definition of significance provides a frame of reference for a gentle and deliberate realignment of your time and resource allocation toward what you consider significant.

Brian Shepler, the CFO for Ronald Blue and Company in Atlanta, Georgia, learned early in his career that many business leaders are out of balance. He didn't want to become one of them—not in his first half of life and certainly not in his second.

At the same time, Brian is far from a limp-wristed, mediocre Christian without drive or ambition. Now in his mid-thirties, he earned an MBA from the University of Chicago Business School, ranked the number three graduate program in the country. Brian worked several years as a Goldman Sachs financial analyst, moved on to a private equity group, and then joined a large asset management firm.

What makes Brian's story stand out above the crowd? Is it that he was an exceptional student or went to a top three business school or spent time at Goldman Sachs? No. What makes

Brian stand out from the rest of his graduating class at Chicago Business School is that, from as early as his mid-twenties, he pursued success in his career with an eye on significance. As one opportunity after another opened up during his first half of life, he found the freedom that comes from charting his own course in a healthy, balanced way. And those choices positioned him well to make a major impact with his life in his second half.

A critical turning point in Brian's life occurred when his mentor was diagnosed with terminal lung cancer. "Instead of him mentoring me up the corporate ladder," Brian says, "he asked me to spend some time with him exploring faith issues. As we talked each day, I could see his health deteriorating rapidly. Just four days before he died, as we sat together, he prayed a believing prayer in the gospel."

Today Brian says that his mentor's passing "had a *tremendous* impact on my professional outlook. He had been the classic absentee father and regretted much about his lack of interaction with his family. I became more passionate than ever about balancing work and family (now that I had one) and began to seek greater purpose in my day-to-day work. Outside of personal relationships, my greatest impact as an equity analyst was potentially aiding a handful of portfolio managers in slightly increasing the alpha in their portfolios. My wife was quick to sense and acknowledge that I needed less time in front of a computer and more time building relationships.

"I saw so many people in my early Wall Street days living dual lives; they were incredibly unhappy. Their jobs were challenging, but you could tell something was missing because they'd approach work and their faith as two separate entities. I've always believed a holistic worldview is the only healthy one."

Because Brian could see the whole picture early on in his first half, he found it easier to pursue success with a clear image of significance in mind. His path to achieving balance got a boost from Bob Buford's *Game Plan*, which helped Shepler know his heart. "The resources available at *www.halftime.org* helped me discover my heart for stewardship, kids, and music," says Shepler. "That helped me focus where my impact will be greatest—plus the relationships developed will be long-term because my heart is in it."

One ministry close to Shepler's heart is a Nashville-based organization that seeks to build character in kids kindergarten through eighth grade. Through its musical approach and curriculum programs, the organization has been able to enter hundreds of public schools and connect with several hundred thousand kids since 1995. It has been particularly effective in schools that have suffered shootings.

Shepler has helped the ministry develop a strategic business plan. "It's fulfilling to help the leaders of that organization operate out of their gifts of creativity and vision casting—to free them up to do what they do best—while people like me help steer them in a positive financial direction," says Shepler.

Being free to focus on what you do best is crucial for those in the first half of life. But with that freedom comes responsibility.

"There are a lot of demands on our time," Shepler explains. "And I believe there's a biblical mandate for us to work hard at this age. But life requires balance. Ultimately, if those in the first half of life are solely devoted to career pursuits and haven't sought a balance that enables the achievement of some eternal return on investment, they often come up way short in the fulfillment category.

"While you may not think you have the time to contribute, if you are up front about what you can and can't bring and the amount of time you have to devote, you can form a successful partnership with a social sector organization," Shepler declares. "Many people have a fear factor about not-for-profit relationships becoming all-consuming. But your partnership with a ministry is most likely to succeed if you are clear about what your role will be, make sure that it matches your heart and skill sets, and get your expectations in writing. With those controls in place, there's freedom that allows people to invest in the social sector more openly."

Today, as CFO for Ronald Blue and Company, a national Christian financial management firm, Brian bring his skills to bear on an organization that combines skillful asset management of over two billion dollars for almost four thousand Christian clients, with the ability to help them use those resources for maximum kingdom impact. Imagine the impact he can have in this world.

Why does it free us to know what we want for a life mission? When we know what we want most out of life, we free ourselves up to let many other good things go undone, many possible dreams go unpursued, many of other people's agendas for our life go unanswered—as we pursue what we know we are called to do.

I speak to groups of people in Halftime all over the country. I always ask them, "How many of you run your business or practice with a mission statement or goals and objectives?" Of course, almost every hand goes up. It's a given that we have a clear mission statement for our business because we know it is the only way to get the entire team focusing on the same outcomes and pulling in the same direction. Then I ask that same crowd, "How many of you have a personal mission statement that incorporates any element of your spirituality?" In most cases, less than 25 percent of the audience answers in the affirmative. Most do not have a personal mission statement.

For most of us, this becomes an "ah-ha!" moment. All of a sudden, it dawns on us that we would not even think of running our business or our law practice or hospital without a mission statement—and yet we go through life without one. A personal mission statement will provide you with clarity, even if you are just approaching Halftime, to be laser-sharp focused on what really matters to you—and then you can intentionally let many other things go.

Planning makes the difference between having a midlife crisis, a deadly boring second half, or one that is the adventure of your lifetime.

Chapter 7

Creating a Playbook

I began my career in the marketing department of a major national bank, a great boot camp for learning basic management skills. In my role at the bank, as well as in my real estate development business, I learned to rely on careful, strategic planning. But at the time it never dawned on me that planning techniques might also apply to my personal life. It seemed a little too uptight to plan my life—perhaps even unspiritual to lay out in black and white what I intended to do with my life. After all, how can God lead someone who already has his mind made up about where he is going and how he is going to get there?

In the late 1980s I was asked to teach an adult seminar at a Christian camp on the topic of planning your life. The camp, located in a beautiful lake district of northern Ontario, featured cold and crisp mornings even in July. The wood fire felt warm and comforting at 8 a.m., but by noon the sun grew hot and you headed for a dip in the crystal clear lake. I felt excited about speaking on life planning, because planning had proven to be such a valuable thing in my own life.

While my thoughts on life planning were still in their infancy, the principles remain timeless. Yet I had a surprise coming. I found a significant disconnect between my audience's view of the Christian life and these biblical concepts of planning. As the presentation part of my session wrapped up and I began to engage the group in dialogue, I felt surprised to discover that some considered planning inappropriate in the Christian life. Others seemed overwhelmed by the idea of life planning. From their perspective, it seemed senseless to try to steer life in a different direction in the face of so many uncontrollable factors and so little wiggle room.

They had this vague notion (one I had earlier shared) that life planning takes the faith out of life. I remember a large man, we'll call him Richard, who owned a truck maintenance business, raising his hand and with real passion saying dogmatically, "How can God lead you spontaneously in life if you have it all written down airtight, planned, and mapped out for the next five years?"

I think what frustrated me most about this reaction was that I knew from experience that planning is the very thing that gives you the flexibility to follow God's leading in a spontaneous way. Planning doesn't diminish God's ability to change your direction. I knew what Richard's life was like—dominated by work—and that unless he became intentional, it would likely continue to be dominated by his work in fifteen years. I knew that much of what he could be doing for God with his talent was getting squeezed out because he was defaulting to growing the business, building the lake cottage, and buying faster jet skis.

There's nothing inherently wrong with any of those, of course, but defaulting to our cultural norm (to what we see modeled by others around us) is risky when you do not have a plan. Of course, there are exceptions. I recently inquired about Richard and what he has done with his life since that summer camp fifteen years ago. I wanted to see if he had found the freedom to follow God in spontaneous ways because he had not planned. Was he available and did he follow spontaneously? What's your guess?

His life today looks like any average fifty-something-year-old business owner in North America. Certainly no signs of bold, spontaneous steps of faith.

On the other hand, another friend of mine, Dave, also declared that day that the idea of planning life seemed outside the bounds of faith. At the time, Dave was starting a software company in Montreal. He was the kind of guy who integrated his faith into everyday life in the marketplace. Dave and his family recently visited us in North Carolina. As we chatted about the past fifteen years, I found it remarkable how dramatically different his life had turned out from that of Richard.

Dave's business has done well. He still allots a significant amount of time to leading it in order to stay at the front edge of the rapidly evolving supply chain management software space. Over the years, however, he discovered that he really wants to help at-risk teens. He and his wife have downsized their lifestyle, moving from the suburbs into the city so the kids they want to serve can get to their home by subway. The high school he helped to start for at-risk teens was featured in the city newspaper as a model for how to make a difference in kids' lives. It has now been serving kids in ninth through twelfth grade for more than ten years. He has reorganized his job description to enable him to spend part of each week working with Youth for Christ.

As Dave and I talked, he laid out a clear plan he had in his mind for his second half. Since then, I have observed Dave carefully implementing the plan, despite many unexpected turns, allowing God's Spirit to direct him along the way.

Ever since that day at camp, I have grown more convinced of the need to challenge people to plan their lives. But I have also become convinced that most people need help with life planning. The ideas need to be simple and doable. They need a solid, biblical foundation for life planning and how planning can dovetail with a life open to God's daily leading.

For many, planning does not come naturally. For some of those summer campers, the concept of planning even their *day*, much less their *week*, felt intimidating. So planning their *life* seemed way out of reach. After all, since we can't control many things in life, how can we plan for them? These folks believe their life is already predetermined in many ways—by their mortgage, the demands of their job, the pressures of running a home and family. In addition, many have never had someone walk them through the tactics of life planning in a way they could begin to implement.

Most of all, I made three big realizations through that experience:

1. We need to begin this discussion with a look at what the Bible says about planning our lives.
2. For those not wired as strategic thinkers, we need to lead them through this process with full room for emotions to engage.
3. We need to help people temporarily set aside all of the legitimate life constraints that keep them from dreaming or being creative.

In my own story, life planning came very naturally. It comes easily. I plan everything. In fact, the most difficult day of the week for me always has been Saturday, because the rest of the family wants to protect Saturday from the stress and obligation of a schedule, while I want to have every minute of the day planned before I can relax. Okay, I know that's not normal. But perhaps my inclination and natural abilities in the area of personal planning will enable me to unpack for you the subtleties and nuances of life planning so that you can experience the big benefits of planning with a minimum of research and effort.

When I could see that our business was becoming successful, Linda and I pushed the pause button on new projects and spent several months developing a strategic life plan. Bottom line, I wanted to ensure that we did not simply default to some expected and perhaps culturally normative life path. Instead, we insisted on discovering a life plan that would enable us to invest part of our time in serving others outside our own immediate family. But frankly, we had no idea what that might be.

It was clear to me from the Bible that God expects us to plan. Proverbs 14 boils it down: "The wisdom of the prudent is to give thought to their ways." It goes on to say "Those who plan what is good find love and faithfulness." I could see how Paul planned his efforts carefully and yet was very open to last minute changes that the Spirit of God would whisper in his ear. In our football analogy it's like coming out of the locker room with a clear game plan but having enough confidence to allow the quarterback of our life to "call an audible" as circumstances change.

Perhaps you love your career, or perhaps you still need to dedicate a large amount of your time to earning an income, but you desire to infuse significance into your life. The desire for significance has to translate beyond feelings to plans and then to action. You will need to be intentional. You need to plan. So how can you begin to plan for the next five years?

God has a plan in mind, but he often does not open it up to us all at once. That does not prevent us, however, from prayerfully beginning to chart out what we believe he has in mind for us in the near future, and then to use that as a guide for our future decisions as new information and opportunities surface.

The prophet Jeremiah experienced this firsthand. He tells us that the word of the Lord came to him, saying "Before I formed you in the womb I knew you, before you were born I set you apart; I appointed you as a prophet to the nations" (Jeremiah 1:5).

Later in his book, Jeremiah declares that God had an intentional plan in mind for his people: " 'For I know the plans I have for you,' declares the LORD, 'plans to prosper you and not to harm you, plans to give you hope and a future' " (Jeremiah 29:11).

Planning for your second half, however, has unique considerations that may not mirror strategic planning for your business or your professional practice—unique considerations vastly different from the career planning you may do in your mid-thirties, and different once again from the planning you will do in your sixties for finishing life well.

At Halftime you have a wealth of knowledge about yourself that you did not have earlier. A lot of water has gone under the bridge and you have had the chance to see where you perform the best, how you react to varying situations, what you are passionate about, and what doesn't turn your crank. If you reflect carefully on your past twenty or more years of life, you may begin to see, for example, how much solitude you need versus team interaction, how creative and unstructured an assignment environment you prefer versus having a clear process or guideline. You now know if you are drawn to large, scalable projects, which are likely to have immense impact, or toward individuals whose lives you can touch personally.

At midlife you are not likely newly wed and focused on having children, but closer to fifty with parents who are aging and need more attention and care. You have multigenerational family issues that must be incorporated into your planning—issues not relevant to your earlier life. You may be wondering how will you leave a legacy through your grandchildren?

In addition, your financial planning will be quite different. Because you are seeking significance in your second half, you may define financial success differently, not in terms of maximum income or fastest capital growth, but rather in terms of sustainable, reliable income generation that frees up part of your time for serving others.

These serve only as illustrations for how life planning in Halftime differs vastly from corporate planning or from planning at other stages of life. If you are not wealthy but desire a significant second half, planning is crucial and yet very challenging. In spending countless hours coaching regular people through Halftime, we have chronicled the top ten issues you need to address in your plan. The next chapter will walk you through those ten components in an effort to make it easy for you to begin, regardless of how much planning experience you have had.

Chapter 8

A Ten-Step Halftime Plan

A significant second half is something like being in a triathlon, where athletes compete in swimming, biking, and running. You will not win if you train only in one area. Instead, you must plan to win in all three areas, or to hold your own in two areas but be way out in front of the pack in the third area. In the same way, a significant second half is built on a playbook that includes all of the important areas of your life, not just your vocational life.

You need a plan for the second half that enables you to be an outstanding husband or wife, parent and grandparent, a wise money manager, and broaden your success beyond your own interests to making a difference in the world around you. These next few pages will enable you to make a great start at crafting that plan. What follows is not comprehensive; many life coaching programs will take you deeper and provide you with a facilitator who can help you to craft an individualized program. The very latest resources we have discovered are listed at the Halftime web site (*www.halftime.org*) under "resources."

For the best results, I encourage you to work through this material in several sittings. First, take an hour and work straight through it, filling in every answer you can. Along the way, identify those areas where you do not have an answer or to which you have never given much thought.

Then take a full-day retreat at some quiet place where you will not be interrupted. Take your Bible, a notepad, and perhaps this book, together with the resources recommended in this chapter. Prayerfully work slowly through this material once again in great detail.

Finally, as you begin to live out your life plan, ask your closest friends for their insights. Come back to it in four to six months; with a little experience under your belt, you can add further improvements.

Step One: Write Down What Makes You Most Passionate

What causes, issues, and groups of people are you most concerned for? What change do you most want to help bring about in the world?

List your top two areas of passion:

_____

_____

Step Two: Pinpoint Your Three Greatest Natural Abilities

You probably have a good idea right now about what your greatest strengths are, but it may be difficult for you to narrow that down to two or three things. I am okay as a manager, but it is not my top strength. It would be tragic for me to invest my life in management when I am much better at strategic thinking. If you cannot definitively pinpoint your top three abilities, then I recommend that you take the time to do a formal assessment.

You can find multiple ability assessment tools on the Internet, such as *www.youruniquedesign.com*, or *www.strengths finder.com*. Just search on your favorite search engine for "abilities assessment test."

Write your top two abilities here:

_____

_____

Step Three: Identify Your Spiritual Gifts

When a person becomes a Christian, the Bible tells us that he or she receives at least one spiritual gift. A spiritual gift is an extraordinary ability intended by God to be used to serve others. Each spiritual gift can be developed.

As I speak with groups of Christians in their forties and fifties, I have discovered that only about a third know their spiritual gift and are actively developing it.

It's easy to discover your spiritual gift today using self-assessment tests available for free on the Internet. Using your preferred search engine, search for "spiritual gifts test" and select two tests you like. Normally these tests will prompt you through one hundred or so questions and then grade you at the end, ranking your responses relative to thousands of others who have taken the same tests. They will provide you with their assessment of your top spiritual gifts. Why take two different tests? You will benefit from a second opinion.

Write your top two spiritual gifts here:

_____

_____

Step Four: Develop Your Personal Mission Statement

Discover the space where your passion, potential, and ability overlap—in other words, your personal calling.

A certain amount of water has to have gone under the bridge of life before we can effectively begin to craft a personal mission statement. Many of us came out of college with very little real world experience and had to make choices about our career, despite our lack of preparation. Halftime provides you with the luxury of twenty or more years of hindsight and experience as the basis on which to craft a mission statement.

According to management guru Peter Drucker, a mission statement is designed to say "why we do what we do. What we want to be remembered for." It is not intended to describe how we will go about it, because tactics change as our environment and technology change.

For most of us, our personal mission statement changes somewhat over time; but key elements are unlikely to change. Three primary elements make up your personal mission statement:

- What kind of people or what cause do you care about the most?
- What difference do you dream that you could make for those people or that cause?
- What is your greatest skill or area of competence that you can bring to bear?

As for myself, I discovered that I care most about two groups of people: successful people who long for more than success; and people seeking a personal relationship with God who have not yet found him. I dream of helping thousands of successful Americans in midlife to reorient their lives to pursue God and his calling on their second half. I dream that their involvement in what God is doing will reach millions of people who are seeking a relationship with God, but have not yet found him.

My greatest strength is in the area of thought leadership. I may be competent in management, but I am not outstanding. I can teach, but only just above average. I have a hard time with empathy and compassion. (I have a "heart mentor" who is helping me grow in this area, but I have so far to go.) Yet I have a superior ability to understand the issues involved in reaching a goal and then helping to shape a strategy that will take the team or individual there.

You may not yet have given your second half enough thought to seriously write a second-half mission statement. Or you may be partway through Halftime, and this may be the missing piece of the puzzle. Either way, your mission statement will likely evolve as you move into your second half. One thing is certain: it will help the process if you make a best effort now and draft or redraft your mission statement.

The easiest way to begin to draft a personal mission statement is to use an equation by combining your gifts, passions, and impact you want to make into a single short sentence. It may feel mechanical, and if so, you will do better simply to begin writing a mission statement in longhand, or drawing a picture of how you envision your second half. From my experience, most need a jump start.

Here's my personal mission statement:

To be a thought leader in mobilizing high capacity leaders for Kingdom impact.

That personal mission statement comes out of a combination of three things:

- My gifts—strategic thinking
- My passions—helping business and professional leaders in midlife transition. I am also passionate about helping people get to know Jesus Christ
- The impact I want to make—to see people in the US and abroad learn about the love and forgiveness of God through Jesus Christ

The temptation is to make the mission statement too comprehensive or too broad. Too comprehensive a mission statement tries to incorporate the perfect blend of all the roles you play: family, marriage, your day job, recreation, and so on. Instead, let your mission statement assume that your second-half plan includes a balance of family time, marriage investment, and work to provide your financial needs. This will free your mission statement up to focus on providing overarching direction for how you will invest your discretionary time, talent, and treasure. An example of a mission statement that is too broad is: "I will follow God and be used by him as he directs." That's a given for all of us who call ourselves Christ-followers. The exercise is designed to enable you to begin to refine what, specifically, God is calling you to do.

Draft your personal mission statement:

_____

_____

_____

_____

_____

_____
_____
_____
_____
_____

Step Five: Define the Position You Best Play on the Team

Most often we'll spend our second half working alongside others who have a commitment to the same things we care about. That's why it is important that your life plan include a clear understanding of the function you play most effectively within an organization: subject expert, process designer, builder, people manager, reliable implementer, administrator, strategist, organizer, marketer, board member, funding partner, social entrepreneur, turn-around artist, team builder, etc.

The best positions for me on the team are:

_____
_____

Step Six: Discover Your Spouse's Goals and Desires

You may already know what your spouse dreams of doing in the second half of his or her life. Most of us, however, have never asked that question of our spouse. So take an evening to go to your favorite spot to hang out and ask your spouse some questions:

- Are there any dreams you had when we were younger that we have let die but that you would like to revisit?
- If our kids were settled in their own homes and adult lives, and if you could use your time however you wanted, what kinds of things do you think would most fulfill you?
- I am working on a life plan for my second half, and I want to make sure, first and foremost, that we plan this together. Would you be willing to do a similar plan for your own second half? I would love to look for ways to

overlap our individual plans to make sure they have an optimum blend of doing life together, with the freedom to pursue and support each other's individual dreams.

What is the single biggest area where your spouse's second-half dreams overlap with your dreams or your areas of passion?

_____

_____

Step Seven: Discover Where Your Life Needs Better Balance

Remember, this is a marathon, not a sprint. To finish well, you need balance in four areas of your personal life. I call those four areas the Four Primary Pillars. They are:

- Faith—a commitment to lifelong spiritual development
- Fitness—to be in top physical shape
- Family—to have a healthy family life
- Friends—loving and growing relationships

Write down the one area you consider weakest and write down two things you will do to help rebalance your life in this area.

I am weakest in this area:

_____

I will make the following two systemic changes to shore up this area so that my second half builds on a firm foundation:

_____

Step Eight: Plan Your Finances with an Eternal Perspective

Without having a financial plan that supports what you want to do in your second half, you will severely limit yourself. You do not have to be financially independent to move from success to significance, but you must have a plan—and it may require sacrifice and intentionality.

An effective plan for you may be surprisingly simple. It needs to define a spending plan designed to support your second-half mission statement and a strategy to generate the necessary level of income, while providing the maximum amount of discretionary time. Assuming that you have some significant savings, as well, your long-term investment strategy may need some adjustments to align it with your life mission.

Depending on your level of assets, you may wish to use a professional financial planner; and if you do, I strongly recommend that you use one such as Ronald Blue and Company, that has a Christian stewardship perspective. Managing your finances with an eternal mind-set is radically different from managing them with the goal of getting the most pleasure out of them before you die or leaving as much for your children as possible.

The most crucial aspects of your financial plan include answers to the following primary questions:

- How much is enough? To what standard of living are you willing to reduce your lifestyle in order to pursue your dreams? How much stuff (material accumulation) is enough?
- How will your family budget need to change to support your second half? You may already have a detailed budget or spending plan. Go carefully through that budget to identify what you feel you can remove, if necessary, in order to pursue what God may be calling you to.

This is where the concept of redefining success meets reality. While we are going to unpack this topic in detail in the chapter on finances, take some time now to put down your initial thoughts about the two preceding questions:

How much is enough? (relative to your present lifestyle)

How will our budget need to change?

Step Nine: Set Five Goals

What are the five most important goals for the next year or two that will prepare you to live out your personal mission statement? Peter Drucker says that "if you have more than five goals, you have none." That's because goals are intended to focus you.

Perhaps you have a goal in the area of physical fitness. Or maybe you have a financial goal, or a spiritual goal in terms of daily devotional time, or a goal to find several serving opportunities within your areas of passion and gifting. Writing them down and sharing them with a friend will enable them to hold you accountable to your aspirations.

Write your five goals here:

_____

_____

_____

_____

_____

Step Ten: How Will You Measure the Results?

If in five years you have been wildly successful in implementing this new life plan and you have moved well into your second half of life, engaged in what you believe to be God's calling for you, then how will you know? What specific indicators can you use as a measuring stick to see how much progress you are making?

It is important to measure your results, both in the areas where you want your life to change (such as health and fitness goals), as well as measuring results relative to your personal mission statement. My personal mission statement forces me to measure how effective I am in thought leadership and in serving people in midlife transition.

Some of my own measuring sticks are numeric: the number of Halftimers I have impacted; time spent doing exercise; personal spiritual development; controlling family expenses; etc.

Others are much harder to assess, such as measuring how I have grown in my ability to communicate intimately with my wife.

Write down three ways you will measure results in your own life:

_____

_____

_____

Chapter 9

Pacing the Game:
The Margin Dilemma

The fast pace of life in our culture has crowded out time for reflection. My closest friend, Randy, is an anesthesiologist. He recently told me that he has almost no time for personal reflection. The more I interact with people all across the country at the Halftime stage of life, the more I have become convinced that his experience is normal.

When I first met Randy, he served as chief of staff of a major regional medical center. He worked long hours, often under intense, life-and-death circumstances. He was on call several nights a week, and when emergencies arose, he might spend the entire night at the hospital trying to save a life, only to go about his normal work the following day.

Outside of work Randy was one of the most committed fathers I know. With four lively children, he had ball games to attend, homework to help with, encouragement and discipline to administer. In addition, he was striving to find a way to authentically live out his faith in his various professional and social circles.

So when and how can he have enough time to pause and look inside or listen to God about how to invest his second half of life? A professional like Randy—or any serious executive in the corporate world—has to dedicate 100 percent of himself to his task, just to keep up with the pack. So if you find yourself in this situation, how can you create margin? If you feel like Randy, then this chapter is designed with you in mind.

As Dr. Richard Swenson says in his book *Margin*, "Margin is the amount allowed beyond what is needed. It is something held in reserve for contingencies or unanticipated situations. Margin is the gap between rest and exhaustion, the space between breathing freely and suffocating. It is the leeway we once had between ourselves and our limits."[1]

Margin is about intentionally uncluttering our lives so that we can begin to reflect on our second half and from that reflection to begin to invest our excess in leveraged opportunities. If you have no margin, then you will have nothing to give away. It has been said that the measure of a great life is not how much it accumulates, but how much it gives away.

Linda and I have made it a priority to discover creative ways to redesign everyday life so that we would have something left over at the end of every day, month, and year. This means extra emotional, physical, financial, and spiritual resources that we can give away in strategic ways to make a leveraged impact in our world.

Margin enables us to do life at a pace that lets us listen to God's calling and direction.

We have to maintain margin in four basic categories of life: the physical, the emotional, the financial, and the spiritual. If you are like me, it feels natural and easy to maintain some margin in at least a few of these areas. Other areas, however, will take serious commitment, creativity, and persistence.

I learned early on how to do this financially. I don't remember a time when I didn't save the money from my birthdays, from lawn mowing, from odd jobs around the house, while my brother Jim (closest in age to me) spent or gave away every last dollar to his name. I have always tended to save rather than to spend. Jim is the kind of caring person who spends freely to make everyday life an adventure; he gives even more freely to those he loves. As a result, it has been relatively easy for Linda and me to create financial margin in life, but for Jim it has taken real work.

Emotional margin is a different story. I had no idea that such a thing as emotional margin even existed, much less understand what changes it would take for me to maintain margin in this area. But I learned early in my second half that without emotional margin, I will simply crash and burn.

I have come close to burning out a couple of times because the serving opportunities that have come across my path feel so exciting and compelling, and I was unaware that my emotional tank was being depleted.

Perhaps, like me, you struggle in one or more of these four areas of margin. The good news is that effective strategies exist to help you regain margin in the areas where you slip. It is essential that you have margin in each of these areas, or the long-term impact of your second half of life will suffer.

If you are out of shape physically, your performance will slip and limit what opportunities you can take advantage of. You may not be able to coach an inner-city little league team and invest in those kids as you would like to, simply because you are out of shape. You may not be able to pursue short-term global mission opportunities, because you can no longer hike to a rural village in South America. You may find your effectiveness drops off midafternoon because you feel sluggish and sleepy. Meaningful conversation with your spouse after 9 p.m. becomes difficult because you'd rather snooze in front of the TV.

Spiritual margin is by far the most subtle of the four. Your second half of life could operate smoothly without spiritual margin. You could even appear to have a productive ministry or service, and yet operate with no spiritual margin. But without spiritual margin, you'll limit the impact of your life and hamper the eternal scope of your influence.

I have to admit, however, that it's not easy to understand what spiritual margin really means. How would I know if I had spiritual margin in my life?

Spiritual margin exists when your heart is so filled with God that it overflows into the lives of others. If my soul is being daily nurtured by time with God to the point that my heart overflows, that overflow is the margin that God can use to bless others around me.

Many books and resources can help us improve in each of these four areas, but we especially need ideas for how a successful, busy person—whose life already seems filled to capacity—can actually do it. We don't need, for example, lots more information about the kind of cardiovascular exercise it takes (thirty minutes, three times a week) to create physical margin; what we need is ideas to help us pull it off.

I have found two critical tactics, both in my own life and in the lives of those who I have coached through Halftime, that can help here. In the next two chapters, we will unpack these ideas—but they begin with gaining a clear assessment of what margins you already have in your life. These will serve you well, regardless of which areas of margin cause you the most struggles.

Assess where you are right now in these four crucial areas: the physical, the emotional, the financial and the spiritual. This is a simple process.

Ask yourself if you have physical energy left over after you meet all of your required responsibilities each day or week. Ask yourself if you have physical capability in excess of what you are currently attempting to do. Is your body in good enough shape, in terms of weight, endurance, flexibility, and strength, to do more than you are currently doing? If not, then you either need to improve your body's ability or your lifestyle is already pushing your body too far. If either is true, it will be hard for you to be physically involved in serving others since you have no physical margin to give away.

Obviously, many of us face illnesses that we cannot cure and that limit our natural abilities. Paul faced this in his second half of life, and yet God used him in amazing ways despite those physical limitations. God, in fact, used those very limitations to keep the apostle dependent on God. But there is nothing "spiritual" about being out of shape and overtired.

Then ask yourself if you feel, at the end of the day or week or month, that you have the emotional energy to care about the needs of others, to spend time with people who need encouragement, to invest your strengths in the lives or ministries that stir your passions outside of your own little world. If you feel completely drained emotionally just by doing life, then you need to make some significant adjustments.

Do you have money left over each month that you currently save, but could use to serve others around you? If not, you will need to develop a plan to spend less or earn more, or both. Without financial margin, you live in survival mode—going from month to month, meeting only your own needs and feeling unable to even begin to think about the needs of others. That situation will completely hamper your ability in your second half to invest in what really matters. In addition, living with no financial margin feels emotionally and physically draining. It compounds the problems you may be experiencing with margin in those other areas.

Last, if you find very little overflow of God's love and grace from your heart to those around you, then you know you have to grow in the area of spiritual margin. If you have not received a card or letter in the past year from someone, thanking you for the encouragement or blessing that you have been to them, then chances are that you have had little spiritual margin to share with others.

Grade yourself on a scale of one to ten in these four areas (ten means you have lots of margin in this area).

Physical _____

Emotional _____

Financial _____

Spiritual _____

Now focus on improving in your two weakest areas. Trying to improve in all four areas at once can feel overwhelming. But if you focus on two areas and give them your full attention, you can make significant progress. In addition, as you gain margin in one area, it becomes easier to gain margin in the other areas.

That's because these areas of margin are intertwined. Lack of margin in one area makes it hard to create margin in another. I have found it far more effective to create margin in one or two areas first, and then use that new margin to enhance your ability to create margin in the others.

Chapter 10

Cutting What Is Least Valuable

Your next step in creating margin is a very simple but difficult task: cutting out the things in life that you consider to be low value. Often this means cutting out what is good to make room for the best. But how can you easily determine what is "the best"? And more importantly, will you have the guts to really cut out the things that are lower value?

Here's how I do this.

As you wrote your mission statement, you settled in your heart and before God what really matters, what you feel is most valuable in life. This exercise will help you assess each of your major activities and responsibilities relative to those factors and then rank them in order of their value to you. The goal is to eliminate the lowest ranking ones, the ongoing roles or responsibilities that do not add enough value relative to better options.

I create a chart like you see in the figure on the following page, where the left column lists all my roles and responsibilities and ongoing activities. The next four columns represent how I rank each of those activities relative to what I consider valuable: Impact (are they changing my world?), Heart (Is it in my areas of passion?), Obligation (Do I have an overriding obligation to do this?), and Growth (Am I growing and developing through this?).

You may choose four completely different column headings based on your mission statement and what you value.

Rank each activity in these four ways, grading them on a scale of one (low value) to five (high value). Add the numbers from left to right and put the sum in the right hand column.

CUTTING LOW VALUE ACTIVITIES					
Activities	Impact	Heart	Obligation	Growth	Total
Coach Soccer	3	2	1	2	8
Habitat for Humanity	4	2	2	3	11

Now rank the activities from top to bottom, with the high number activities at the top. Select the bottom two or three activities and unapologetically eliminate them from your life.

Life changes, and you will need to do this (or something similar) regularly and cull out the things that are no longer best. I recently did this and found that leading a Sunday night couples' small group in my home was a good thing but was not making a very leveraged impact and was not in my area of passion. At the same time, several other men in the group could lead it just as well as I could. So I felt no sense of obligation to continue. I was no longer growing in that role, because I had done it for five years. It landed on the bottom of my list, so I handed it off right away to someone else. That never would have happened if I had not done this exercise because it was not easily apparent that leading this small group was a low value investment.

By not investing time in leading that small group, however, I have opened up several more hours a week to personally coach Halftimers (go to www.LloydReeb.com). Through phone calls, lunches, and emails, I have been able to see one after another discover their calling for the second half of their lives and begin to pursue significance. They are changing their world for the better. I can't tell you how glad I am that I have learned to regularly eliminate some good activities to make way for the best!

Of course, what is best for me may not be what is best for you. Only you can make these assessments, but you need to and to cut the low value activities.

You may do this exercise and come away saying, "I can't just cut that activity." Sure, if parenting or being a husband shows up on the bottom of the list, you may not be able to cut it; but most others you can, if you make up your mind. I actually make a deal with myself before I do the exercise, that the bottom three activities are going to go. I do this because I know it will be hard, and I have to force myself to take the hard steps. But in the long run, it's worth it.

Chapter 11

Overlapping What Is Most Valuable

Chances are that if you have ranked your activities and cut several of the lowest value ones, you are feeling much "lighter." You're traveling through life with far less luggage.

Linda and I recently attended a three-day conference in Florida. For the last leg of our flight we rode on a little plane from Tampa to Naples. Partway through, a couple behind us asked if we were heading to the same conference they were going. Sure enough, we were.

They had noticed the book my wife was reading and guessed we might be part of the conference. We agreed to ride to the hotel together (actually, they had reserved a very nice, large car, so we freeloaded on them). What happened next I found unbelievably funny.

Linda and I walked off the plane, each with one small carry-on suitcase for the four days. Once they had collected all their bags, their luggage consisted of four very large suitcases and three smaller handbags. We packed the trunk, packed the center of the back seat, and carried suitcases on our laps just to get it all into the car. We joked about how they must have just emptied their closet into their suitcases. They felt so embarrassed, but all in fun. Of course, every time we saw them that weekend, they had on yet another lovely outfit, and lots more to choose from if the weather changed. Linda and I had a few interchangeable outfits, and wore the same socks and underwear all weekend (just kidding).

As we packed for that trip, we purposely edited what we took with us so that we could focus on enjoying our time together rather than on the stuff. For example, when we first arrived at the hotel, we spent almost no time unpacking, ironing clothes, choosing outfits, or changing clothes. Instead, within minutes we hit the beach. You see, Linda and I had decided up front that we wanted to enjoy the time and activities and not get bogged down in having the most appropriate outfit for every possible setting. If we didn't have it with us, then there was no way it could commandeer our time and attention.

We can take the same approach in the broader landscape of life.

When you cut the good in order to focus on the best, you sacrifice some things but gain so much more. We did not go around the hotel naked; we simply made each outfit serve multiple purposes.

My point? We need to do the same thing in life if we are serious about creating margin.

Reflect on the activities that have ranked highest in the exercise in the last chapter. What creative ways can you overlap those activities to save time, money, and energy? How can you make one activity or one time allocation accomplish two or three important things?

Consider how it plays out in my life:

I have only a few non-negotiables in my life. No matter what happens, I am committed to being a nurturing husband, an involved parent, a very close friend to a few other guys, and using my gifts well. But beyond that, the rest is negotiable.

Given my personal mission statement ("To be a thought leader in mobilizing high capacity leaders for Kingdom impact"), the best activities in which I believe I can invest my time, energy, and money are understanding and serving people in Halftime and organizations that serve them. In addition, since I have a high degree of passion for helping spiritual seekers explore a relationship with God, I need to be personally involved in helping non-Christian friends find their way to God. In the mix, I somehow need to stay in shape physically, or otherwise poor health and lack of stamina will deter me in the areas of life that really matter.

Add to this equation the fact that I gain energy from being alone (that is the formal definition of an introvert), and therefore I need solitude to maintain my sanity. I also need reflective time with God each day. I need to eat three meals a day, and so on. So how can I overlap these needs and activities to open up margin in my life? All of these things are important, but how can one person possibly fit all of them into a normal week without going crazy or without being mediocre in all of them?

Consider a few specific things that might enable someone with my set of values to pursue these things and still have some margin in life:

Idea 1: I need to discover an activity that combines cardiovascular exercise three times a week with prayer, and that also provides me with the solitude I need to maintain emotional margin.

Solution 1: I bike three times a week by myself, without my cell phone. I discipline myself to pray and reflect during my bike ride.

Idea 2: I travel a lot, speaking about Halftime issues. Sometimes my trips occur when my kids can travel with me. I am committed to making lasting memories with my children. When my children were preteens, I realized that it was important to do something special to mark the passage in their life from child to teen.

Solution 2: As I looked for ways to combine all of these activities into one overlapping experience, I discovered that, with a little planning, as each child turned thirteen I could include them on a speaking trip and make it a very special memory at the same time.

When Carter turned thirteen, I had to travel to Dallas—so I included him on that trip. By staying over a Saturday night, the total cost of both flights came to less than the cost of a single flight on Friday. We stayed in a nice hotel downtown and enjoyed the best of Texas, including the Fort Worth Rodeo. We ate buffalo meat. Stayed up late. Laughed and joked.

Today, if you go into his bedroom, you will find a large photo on the wall taken by the room-service lady the morning of his birthday. I noticed that the menu allowed children up to thirteen to order any item off the breakfast menu for just a few dollars. In a rare moment of genius, I ordered for him everything on the room service breakfast menu. The memory will last forever. He had pancakes and strawberries, eggs and bacon, hot cereal, muffins, fruit. All served on a rolling table with a rose and a linen tablecloth. The whole weekend cost me very little extra time and money above what I would have had to spend on the ministry assignment. But it was priceless.

My daughter, Caroline, loves design and fashion. When she turned thirteen, she joined me on a ministry trip to San Francisco. I had to rent a car, so we spent a few dollars more and rented a convertible, then drove over the Golden Gate Bridge with the top down—just making memories. We ran along the bluffs overlooking the ocean at Big Sur. We window-shopped in Carmel-by-the-Sea. I had to travel all the way there and back anyway, but this made the trip a win-win for ministry and family, all in one.

Idea 3: I find it important to take an annual spiritual retreat, at least several days away from my normal surroundings to reflect on where God is leading me and what he might want to teach me in the coming year. I also have a desire to be involved somewhere in God's global efforts. It's hard, however, to find the time for this kind of international travel. So I began to look for a way that I could overlap an annual spiritual retreat with an overseas speaking trip. How could these overlap?

Solution 3: In my role as a pastor, I have ongoing experience in helping people to explore Christianity and in training others to share their faith in a winsome way. At the same time, the foreign mission agency I have worked with has a need to facilitate interactive group discussions among its missionaries, to reenergize them for personal evangelism, and to help them think outside the box and develop new strategies. So I travel overseas each year to teach evangelism. This kind of global travel provides large chunks of time for spiritual retreat. I combine spiritual retreat time and leverage my ongoing learning about evangelism at the church. This single, creative step has enabled me to pursue several needs in my life with only one trip.

Idea 4: I need a few very close intimate friendships, people who know me well and have the freedom to tell me what they see happening in my life even if I don't want to hear it. I need to know I have a few people who love me and are committed to me regardless of what I do. At the same time, part of emotional renewal and recharge for me comes through competition and aggressive sports activities. How can I overlap these activities?

Solution 4: My friend, Randy, loves tennis and weight lifting. By committing to play tennis or work out together regularly, I can accomplish two important things.

Idea 5: I am committed to staying engaged in helping non-Christians discover a relationship with God through Jesus Christ. At the same time, I need to eat three meals a day.

Solution 5: I can choose to eat these meals by myself or with whoever comes along, or I can strategically aim to eat lunch with people I know to be open to pursuing God.

These are just a few examples. My life is certainly far from perfect in terms of margin, and these ideas for overlapping activities may not come close to working in your life. So instead I ask you to use them as thought-provoking examples as you consider your own list of activities, looking for creative ways to overlap the very "best" activities.

As you do, you will create margin in your life.

After a year, reassess where you are and begin again. Margin will gradually disappear over time, unless you regularly reassess your activities relative to your current values.

There are seasons of life, just as Halftime is a season at midlife that brings changing opportunities. Your circumstances change, providing new and perhaps better opportunities—and some good opportunities fade away over time. You change, your skills increase, enabling you to take on more leveraged opportunities. Your values change and new areas of personal growth emerge.

It is essential to regularly reassess your activities in this or some similar way. I suggest annually.

Perhaps you feel you are too busy or tired or drained to even begin to create margin.

Perhaps you just went through the exercise of cutting the good to free up margin for the best, only to find that you are too busy, overcommitted in your career, too much in debt, or too tired to actually implement it. In either case, you may feel tempted to set this book down and forget all about redefining success and pursuing significance.

Let me encourage you! I have coached people in midlife who feel just like that, and I've seen them slowly emerge with real margin in life and ultimately discover avenues to significance. Today they are making a difference in their world and having a blast doing it—against all odds.

You can too.

Chapter 12

You Are a Free Agent—
and It's Legal to Negotiate

In your corporate or professional life you commonly try to negotiate win-win solutions. If you have achieved some measure of success by midlife, chances are that you know how to negotiate well. It may be that your negotiating skills are the most critical ingredient to creating margin in your personal life.

No one is going to come up to you with creative strategies for how to open up margin in your life. Only *you* can do that.

After seventy years of tightly controlled central planning in communist Albania, most residents no longer believed they could change their circumstances through negotiation. I saw with my own eyes that the Albanian farmers did not believe they could change their situation, and as a result, they did not negotiate with those who controlled the transportation of their goods, the prices for their produce, or the flow of water to their fields.

If you are going to negotiate win-win arrangements that will enable you to pursue significance in your second half of life, you need to believe that you can. Few things feel more rewarding to me than to advise individuals in Halftime to negotiate: with their employer, with their employees, with their spouse and children, with their church, with their investment manager, with their home maintenance people, with the ministries they are considering for some kind of partnership.

But to negotiate, you need to know what you want and believe that if God is behind it, he can make the impossible happen. You need to clearly communicate what you believe to be

God's calling in your life and what you consider to be valuable—without blinking at the consequences.

When you ask for specific, unique arrangements, there's a risk, of course, that the people you are negotiating with will misunderstand you. It could come across as if you consider yourself something special, someone who deserves special treatment. The fact is, you are something special and God has some special things for you to do. But you will never get on with those special things if you spend the rest of your life bound by other people's agendas. If your longing is limited to paying off a big mortgage on a house that society says you need; paying for trips you felt pressured to take and clothes your family just *had* to have, working late every night because its part of the corporate culture. You are a free agent. You need to feel the freedom to negotiate with those you love and those you work with to create what you really need.

When I needed more time to pursue the serving opportunities that today make my second half so exciting, I negotiated with my business partner. We agreed together to pay him a portion of gross revenue on our buildings and have him pick up my management responsibilities. The ministry I wanted to work with is located in Detroit, and I did not want to live there, so I negotiated with the organization to telecommute; I agreed to visit the office six times a year. When I discovered that I need a blend of "thinking" work and "life-on-life" work, I renegotiated to spend part of my time as a pastor in our church, working life-on-life with people. When my travel schedule became too intense, I negotiated with Linda to find a balance of travel that she can live with (no more than seven days a month) and which still enables me to speak anywhere in the world on topics I care about.

Without careful, prayerful negotiation, I never would have discovered any of these win-win solutions. Remember, you are a free agent and you take your direction first and foremost from God. So negotiate to your heart's content!

Taking the initiative and negotiating the primary elements of your life, such as your finances and the level of lifestyle you will enjoy, enables you to find freedom to live your second half as you desire.

But first, you need to decide how much is enough.

Chapter 13

Where Is the Financial End Zone?

How much is enough?

Not many of us have the financial freedom to leave our job or sell our company at midlife. More importantly, judging from the experiences of dozens of others who have bailed out of their careers, I'd have to say that seldom is it healthy to just quit work and abruptly jump into untested ministry waters.

Unless you decide how much is enough when it comes to your finances, however, it is highly unlikely that you will be able to break free from the gravitational pull of your first-half success.

I discovered that enough was never enough. I am sure you have discovered the same thing. At every level of income and wealth accumulation, we think that just attaining the next level will give us the security and freedom we need and desire. But when we reach that level, we just raise the bar. We look over the fence and the grass once again looks greener on the lawn of the guy who earns just a little more or has a little more savings.

I can remember feeling that if I could just save up enough to buy a home . . . then if I could just pay off the mortgage . . . then if we lived on the water and I could sail—*then*, at last, I'd feel content. At each stage I quickly raised the bar of satisfaction. Yet the Bible clearly says, "Godliness with contentment is great gain" (1 Timothy 6:6). The funny thing is, I *was* seeking great gain—but I had not yet come to the point where I felt willing to pursue God and be content with what he had already provided.

The bottom line: I had not decided how much was enough.

Every real estate deal I ever made, from small to large, my dad advised against. Too risky. You see, he was raised on stories of the Great Depression and the risk of losing everything seemed unwarranted to him. I simply could not understand his viewpoint. What motivated me most was the thrill of taking the next hill, the challenge to reach the next financial goal. Each goal reached just led to another goal.

But when I finally called and told him I had decided that enough was enough—that I was not going to build any more buildings, but instead would allocate part of my time to ministry—he completely surprised me by recommending that I do at least one more project. He thought we needed the security of a little bigger nest egg.

As he spoke, I realized that I had a similar desire. I too wished I had a little more financial security. And *then* I would follow God's prompting on my life.

That's when Linda and I decided that enough really was enough. It seemed all too clear to me that if I did not draw a line in the sand, there might never come a time when I felt enough was enough—and in all my gaining, I would have forfeited the most valuable thing of all: the opportunity to follow God, in faith, to do what he had for me to do.

I have come to realize that financial security is a myth. The only real security is found in following what God has in mind for your life. Assets can vanish overnight. Health can disappear and with it our earning capabilities. Inheritances may get gobbled up in nursing care for our parents.

You and I must decide, on our own before God, exactly how much stuff and how much income is enough.

For three years after I decided enough was enough, Linda and I cut our family's living expenses. Now, don't clock out on me; I know that may not be possible in every family. But we learned something that I believe is transferable to most, if not all, families. Every time we cut what we considered low-value expenses to pursue higher-value things, our family's happiness actually *grew*. We discovered parks and libraries, hiking and biking—all of them free. We discovered that many of the most enjoyable things in life are free, and that with a little discipline, we could eliminate low-value expenses and have more fun at the same time.

Many "regular people" ask how they can reconfigure their lifestyles and begin this reflective and investigative process. The reality is, most high-capacity leaders and successful professionals are not financially independent and cannot just walk away from their work. Nonetheless, with discipline, a willingness to be creative and to negotiate win-win scenarios, they can achieve a much higher level of flexibility than they ever dreamed.

Linda and I found that we have more options and greater flexibility than we ever thought. And many others have discovered the same thing. So can you.

Chapter 14

Experimenting with Different Plays and Positions

I had a lot of trouble figuring out the answer to one key question: Was there really a place where I could make a big difference on God's team? Was there a role I could play with my skills that would change my world and create a lasting legacy?

Finding that role would turn out to require as much creativity, initiative, and persistence as developing real estate.

As our first five-year plan unfolded, I began to investigate ministry opportunities that I thought might interest me once I got ready to reallocate part of my time. I investigated more than thirty ministries and found it very hard to gain entrance. Surprisingly, the staff of most of these major Christian organizations had little or no understanding of what a real estate developer does or how they could use my skills. They seemed to feel swamped with administrative work, so they sent me the standard "junk mail" responses that they send to every inquiry, without making the effort to understand what I had to offer them or what I was really looking for. I got the sense they were trying to find an easy fit for me, into an off-the-shelf service opportunity. They seemed largely uncreative, or at least unwilling to put their creativity to work, to find or create an assignment for someone who was not their standard seminary-grad applicant.

I sent my resume to more than thirty-five national ministries, and today I have a file full of the most absurd replies. For example, one ministry suggested that I join a team of carpenters building a ministry center in South America. I learned from that suggestion that they had absolutely no idea what a real estate developer does. I don't even know what end of a hammer to hold, much less how to build a building. Go figure. It simply made me angry.

Leander Rempel, a senior executive with an international mission agency, stood out among the organizations I approached. He listened carefully to my longing to put my skills into play in direct ministry. He asked about my personal strengths, abilities, and interests. Then he invested the time to envision how my skills could help his organization.

I will never forget the feeling of excitement when I read his words in his first letter back to me: "It was good talking to you on the phone on Wednesday night. As I indicated to you, I believe that we have a place for you to exercise the gifts God has given you." He then recommended three separate opportunities and explained why my investment of time would make a leveraged impact.

I knew I could make a difference in the marketplace, but I really wasn't sure if I was needed in the ministry world. Have you ever felt that way? You approached your pastor with an idea and he brushed it off and instead asked you to teach a Sunday school class—and you don't even like teaching kids. Maybe you approached the leader of a major inner-city ministry to ask about how you could be of service, and all she wanted to talk about was the group's funding need for a transitional housing project.

Recently I had lunch with a friend, we'll call him Rick, a seasoned financial planner who is in Halftime. He called to talk about something that felt missing in his life. Rick has a lovely wife, wonderful kids, and a great career, but a significant downturn in the stock market had caused him to wonder how much control he really had over his clients' investments. Were his best efforts making much difference in the world? In the context of that question, he realized he was really searching for second-half significance.

Rick can't just quit his job, nor does he feel called to. But he can carve out ten hours a week. After several meetings over six months, listening to Rick's interests and understanding how he is wired, I asked if he would lead the Community Care ministry at our church. His analytical and leadership skills combined uniquely with his care for hurting people to make him the perfect candidate. At the same time, the church could not afford to hire someone full-time with his caliber of leadership skills.

I suggested that the church hire him for ten hours a week to provide leadership for this entire ministry, with the flexibility to work from his corporate office. We would surround him with administrative help, as well as with tier-two leaders that we can afford to hire full-time, and he would be free to dream and lead and grow this ministry—a ministry dear to his heart.

As I described this idea to him, his eyes filled with emotion, and he choked back his partially chewed burrito. "I am overwhelmed that you would consider me for this role and that you would create an opportunity like this that matches my life situation," he said.

I saw in his face what I had felt more than ten years earlier when I got Leander's letter.

Not every organization is going to understand you or be willing to be as creative as we were for Rick. But there is an organization that will.

Leander willingly took a risk on me and let me test-drive several projects. I completed a home-office relocation study to determine the optimal location for their new headquarters. I led the Albania farmers' project that I described in chapter one. One year I traveled with him to Spain for several weeks to help in the initial planning for the development of a retreat center for drug rehabilitation in Madrid.

These assignments ran parallel with my real estate development career and provided an overwhelming sense that God really could use me to make a significant impact, using my skills, natural abilities, and passions. And I could do so without quitting my job or selling my business!

My heart was captivated by their vision for a rehabilitation retreat center to serve drug users in urban Madrid. But—discovering firsthand that I could use my real estate skills to play a small part in making that rehabilitation center a reality felt thrilling to me.

It is important to test the waters before you jump in. Certain research techniques will save you many hours of time as you investigate opportunities and will help you set clear guidelines with the organizations you investigate.

Finding your niche on God's team is not like finding a new job when your present one grows stale. There are some very distinct differences. We have talked about how ministry organizations often do not understand you and your skills, or how they can be put into play within their organizations. Second, you probably do not understand their work well enough to see the underlying opportunities. That takes more than just reading their brochures and webpage, more than talking to their frontline people. You need to find a way to really wrestle with the opportunities and challenges that they face. And as you do, you will begin to discover a niche for yourself.

Enoch Kerr is a senior who lives in one of our buildings. This man follows God. Before I had even begun a formal search for a ministry assignment, he asked me to join him one Tuesday night to visit a prison. I had never been to a prison before. When I asked him what I would be doing, he simply said, "Come and see." We showed up, cleared security, and visited a number of men with whom Enoch has been building relationships. He led a short Bible study and then we left.

As we were leaving, I felt my heart deeply stirred about the needs of the thousands of men locked up, surrounded by evil and darkness. He too sensed God's Spirit working in my heart and encouraged me to come weekly to visit these men, to try to share God's love in genuine, practical ways. As I did, I discovered two things.

First, I quickly learned that I was not designed to serve criminals. I had no understanding of their world and had trouble relating with them in a way that they perceived as credible.

Second, I discovered a deep, unavoidable longing to take the gospel to people who have never heard about Jesus. That prison ministry experiment taught me two important things that I simply would not have learned by sitting at home or in the church pew. In fact, it affects how I choose to spend my time today.

Just the other day a woman named Tracy called and asked to see me at the church office. She grew up in a wealthy family in an affluent suburb of New York City, with every need provided for except for any element of spirituality. She has no memory of church. She went once in kindergarten, she thinks, but now in her early forties, she is searching for meaning in life—meaning beyond playing tennis every day; meaning when relationships in life don't turn out as planned; meaning when purpose otherwise eludes her.

So she showed up in my office to ask me to explain Christianity to her. In her words, "Would you please start at the beginning for me?" So we spent several hours answering her questions about the Christian faith. This is a role I was designed to play. I am completely at home helping someone through this exploratory journey without them feeling pressured or awkward.

So I choose to serve in this space as a part of the blend of how I allocate my time. I have the privilege of explaining the whole story of Jesus and his life and love to people who have never heard any of it before. I have the thrill of seeing the lights go on in their mind and heart as they understand why he came, what his offer of pardon is all about, and what it would look like to have a genuine relationship with God.

Last week I got a note from Tracy. "First of all," she wrote, "thank you for spending so much time with me a *few* weeks back. It was very helpful. It took me a long time to get through the first five pages of John (the Gospel); it was a hard style to read. However, believe it or not, everything clicked into place on Easter Sunday!!"

Now, stop and think about that. What I learned through that prison ministry experiment helped me choose a serving opportunity that includes communicating the gospel to people who have never heard it. As a result, I had the privilege of helping this lady come to know God and forever change her eternal destiny. I cannot think of anything more significant than that—nor anything more exciting.

There are far more combinations and permutations for how you can serve than you can imagine. My friend, Rick, for example, felt totally surprised that we would cut him loose to lead a major ministry at the church, directly in his area of passion: serving people in crisis, using exactly the amount of time he had available within the context of his career. One man I know who owns an insurance agency goes to China every January to teach Western-style sales techniques and, in the process, has endless opportunities to share his faith in a country closed to traditional missionaries. How many of us have thought about using our four weeks of vacation to make such an interesting contribution? Every time he comes home completely rejuvenated and ready to go again. It's an adventure combined with real impact.

Pat is the finance manager at a large car dealership. When I discovered that he worked from 9:00 a.m. to 9:00 p.m. five days a week, I asked why he had to be there twelve hours straight. He explained that he needs to be "on hand" when a car financing deal must be negotiated or approved. He has a lot of "down time" when a deal is not happening. After helping him define his gifts and passions, we designed a unique ministry role for him. We created an opportunity to lead a significant ministry that required a lot of email and phone coordination, which he can easily do between deals from his office.

Finding your niche on God's team is different from conventional job searches because by midlife we have become specialists and experts in our marketplace role. We often launch out into the wide world of ministry, however, with only a general idea of what we want to do and even less of an understanding of the needs. We are beginning an exploration process, and it will take several tries before we discover a suitable niche.

Joe, my EMS friend whom I mentioned earlier, tapped me on the shoulder one morning at church to ask if we could have lunch. He is in his early forties and, frankly, knows just about everything there is to know about leading the emergency medical services for a major city. Since taking the job in 1997, Joe has reduced the response times to emergency calls from sixteen minutes to just over nine minutes, and the cost per response call has dropped to less than the 1997 tax subsidy—all while the number of yearly responses has jumped from 35,000 to 72,000. Talk about significance! His work has saved hundreds of lives. And yet he longs for more. He wonders if he was created to do something that he just has not yet discovered. His next logical career move might be to take a job as CEO of Medic for an even larger city, or launch his own company where the EMS is privatized. Instead, Joe is taking this opportunity to explore wider than just going higher within his present industry.

As Joe begins to search for a serving role, the thousands of options make his head swim. But he also feels a tremendous sense of freedom and possibility when he considers how many right answers there may be for him. With the limited time he has to dedicate to this search, however, what can he do quickly to narrow the possibilities to the most exciting and leveraged?

Joe faces three primary decisions, the same as you. He (and you) must:

1. Find the right stadium. In other words, in which arena will you serve: the marketplace, your church, your community, international organizations?
2. Find the right spot on the team.
3. Find the model for serving that best fits.

Let's look next at each of these, in turn.

Chapter 15

Finding the Right Stadium

Four primary arenas provide opportunities for second-half service that yield eternal significance. You can serve:

- in the marketplace
- in your church
- in your community
- around the world

Some people create a unique combination of two or more of these. This is the broadest question you must answer as you begin to find your place to serve. You already know what it would look like to serve in the marketplace with more spiritual intention. One way to assess the other three arenas is to find a single serving opportunity in each one and test it. After you sort this out, you will be able to begin to discover your best position on the team.

The Bible is clear that the church is the vehicle God is building to change the world. The church is the hope of the world. It's equally clear from the Bible that God wants to use your church first to change the lives of people in your immediate area, then to change your surrounding community in real, practical ways as you reach out as a family of faith. Ultimately he wants to use your church to change the world as you take the message and compassion of Jesus to other countries.

So, in theory, you could serve in any of these arenas through your own church and under its leadership. In my view, this is the healthiest and most biblical model. In the perfect world, you would belong to a church that not only helps you work through the many spiritual and emotional issues in Halftime but also links you to a wide array of serving opportunities. I describe that kind of church as "Halftime Heaven."

A Halftime Heaven church has a plan in place to thoughtfully prepare you and pave the way for you to explore a scope of serving opportunities: in your work, in the congregation, in the community, or around the world. Such a church casts a vision for the impact you could make. It helps you assess your gifts and passions; connects you to a small group of peers to process the issues; facilitates deeper discussion between you and your spouse on midlife issues; allows you to test a variety of serving opportunities; and ultimately lets you use your leadership skills to really lead.

But let's get real! You may be in a church that simply does not welcome your significant involvement. Sure, it welcomes your tithe and will gladly assign you to some kind of committee so you feel involved. But you know that would kill you. Frankly, the pastor might well feel threatened by your leadership skills; he fears that you will take the vision and strategy and steer off in a different direction. He may worry that you will not come as a humble servant or that you will refuse to be accountable. The church may be bureaucratic and inflexible. So what do you do then?

Or perhaps you attend a church that is really interested in helping you discover your gifts and passions, to sort out midlife issues of balancing work and family life—but when it comes down to it, it offers little scope for real serving. You could teach a Sunday school class, be an elder, join some kind of committee, or volunteer in youth ministry. But to really take a big project and lead—you can see it just isn't going to happen.

Or again, maybe you are in an entrepreneurial church where leaders can lead, where you see a big, compelling vision and tons of significant serving opportunities—but no one seems to know how to help you in this journey of discovering where to plug in and how to make it fit with everything else you have going on.

Four radically different kinds of churches, aren't they? So how does that affect which stadium or arena you play in?

The Bible talks about beginning close to home, then serving the wider region, and ultimately looking to needs around the world. You may find your heart drawn to international missions, but if you have never shown an interest in serving your own local church, it is clear from Jesus' words in Acts 1:8 that you need to begin there. Sometimes, however, your church provides no stadium where you can play.

Defining the kind of church you are in will go a long way toward helping you decide which of these four arenas to serve in. In Halftime, you need two primary things from your church: (1) a wide scope of service opportunities so that you can find one that really fits and (2) some important assistance in the Halftime journey. I call these two key factors the "Serving Scope" and "Halftime Helps." Serving Scope includes not only the variety of ministries within which you can serve but the willingness of the church to let you really lead and create in that space. The Halftime Helps includes vision casting for a significant second half, books, classes, small group opportunities, gifts assessment tools, financial planning help, midlife marriage resources, coaching, and so on.

Look at the "Halftime-Friendly Church Grid" on the next page and determine where your church is. I have been in a Halftime-Hostile church, which ranks low in both factors. Yet despite that handicap, I was able to supplement the scope of my serving opportunities by looking outside the church while still remaining under its authority. I have been in churches and consulted with churches that are in both the Just-Jump-In and the All-Dressed-Up-but-Nowhere-to-Serve categories. I am now a pastor at a church that aspires to the rarefied ranks of Halftime Heaven, and all the challenges that go with that aspiration. I have interacted with other pastors and church leaders in each of these quadrants, and I will give you the best learning I have about how to pursue Halftime in the context of each of them.

THE HALFTIME-FRIENDLY CHURCH GRID

High

Just Jump In	**Halftime Heaven**
This church offers Half-timers a wide array of serving opportunities and little organizational hindrance to their involvement, but very little proactive help in their Halftime journey.	This church provides outstanding tools and coaching and unlimited opportunities to lead.
Halftime Hostile	**All Dressed Up but Nowhere to Serve**
This church provides very little vision, tools or coaching for Halftimers and there are few places where they can serve in significant leadership roles.	This church provides tools, coaching and pathways to Halftimers but there is a limited scope of serving opportunities.

Halftime Helps (X Axis) — Low / High

Low

Halftime Serving Scope (Y Axis)

The Halftime-Hostile Church

Let's start with the worst case—which is that you're in a Halftime-Hostile church. I recommend that you either find another church with a deeper vision for changing the world for Christ or begin to look for opportunities in Christian ministries in your community. As you discover and engage in ministry in your community, you may get interested in serving overseas; but by beginning at home, you can learn from the experience and debrief the experience with your closest friends.

Short-term, international mission trips are a great way to begin. Still, they need to lead to something that you can do in a sustainable way. When Jesus suggested to his disciples that they move from "Jerusalem to Judea to the uttermost parts of the world," I believe he was emphasizing the big idea of beginning to be fruitful where God has you today. It is all too easy to fly around the world for God but never even know our immediate neighbors or get involved in seeing them come to know the Lord. Find the Halftime Helps you need at *www.halftime.org*.

The-All-Dressed-Up-but-Nowhere-to-Serve Church

If your church is "all dressed up, but nowhere to serve," then you will find a lack of real serving opportunities. I suggest that you sit down with your pastor or a senior staff leader with enough leadership clout to really affect the church structure, and explain that you need a wider scope of serving opportunities. Be prepared to describe your gifts, your mission statement, and the role you would like to play in ministry. Ask what he or she suggests you do to widen the scope of serving opportunities.

There is great potential for you to find a good serving role through a church like this, so long as you are willing to begin with a servant's heart and work with the leadership to negotiate the kind of role that fits you best. The Bible is full of examples of the need to be willing to begin at the foot of the table, where the greatest need exists, with a towel over your arm. Consider the profound words of Jesus: "The greatest among you will be your servant. For whoever exalts himself will be humbled and whoever humbles himself will be exalted" (Matthew 23:11–12).

When our family first began attending the church where I now serve as a pastor, it was a young church, still meeting in a school. I remember taking my son, Carter, who was eight at the time, and going on Saturday afternoons to mop the gym floor and set up chairs for the Saturday night service. I wanted a place where he and I could serve beside each other so that he would have a model of what it means to sacrifice what you value (Saturday free time) so that others can come to know Jesus. I wanted him to learn the meaning of what King David wrote: "How can I offer to the LORD that which cost me nothing?" (2 Samuel 24:24). In the process, however, I had the opportunity to serve in an area of immediate need and at the same time had my heart and motives tested in preparation to take on very significant responsibilities.

On the other hand, it is wise to remember the parable of the talents in Luke 19:11–27. The Master required that his servants invest what they had been given and he expected to see real results. The servant who in fear hid his resources in a safe place, unwilling to put it at risk, showed no results at the end of the day. I cringe at the idea of burying my unique gifts under the unwillingness to work hard in my church to find the most leveraged serving role for me.

If your church cannot create a place where you can serve, you are still responsible for investing your talents and resources. If you are in a small church where no significant role exists for you, you will need to explore opportunities outside of church, perhaps in a parachurch ministry, a compassion ministry, or a foreign mission or relief organization. I believe the Bible teaches that wherever you end up serving, you are still accountable to your local church and its authority. The best scenario, if you choose to serve in a ministry outside of your church, is to do so with the support of your church leadership. Its leaders should be praying for you and offering support and accountability—and you should open up your life to their input and critique.

The Just-Jump-In Church

The risk here is that you will get engaged in a fun and challenging ministry without processing many important aspects of Halftime. There may be missing elements of your spiritual life, marriage issues that never have been addressed, or sin patterns that have gone unchallenged. They may not help you create the margin you need to take on this new role, and your family or career may suffer in the process. You may do your second-half ministry with the same rugged individualism that made you successful in your first half. Not healthy.

Ultimately, your second-half impact may be severely hampered by doing the right ministry in the right place with the right preparation. You may find yourself serving in your own strength. If you do not grow closer to God and to those you are serving as a result of your Halftime journey, that is a sign that some of the Halftime Helps are missing.

You need to supplement the Halftime Help your church offers. I recommend that you find or create a small group of peers with which to process many of the Halftime soul issues, while you begin your serving opportunity. Most of the ministries that provide these Halftime Helps, both within and outside of the local church, are listed under "Resources" at *www.halftime.org*. At the very least, I recommend that you obtain the *Success to Significance* video-based small-group curriculum and ask five to ten peers to walk through that six-week process together (available at your Christian bookstore, Lifeway, or *www.halftime.org*).

Community and International Opportunities

No matter your skills or desires, serving opportunities that match you exist in both your local community and around the world. Thousands of overseas opportunities exist: part-time, full-time, and short projects. The Internet provides an excellent portal to begin your research. Search on *www.halftime.org* for a wide variety of real job opportunities in well-run ministries. One site, *www.finishers.org*, compiled more than seventy leading international ministries with specific opportunities for people in Halftime. This site enables you to profile yourself, your interests, and restrictions, and it matches you against thousands of real opportunities, finally returning to you a list ranked by best match.

When I led the Albanian farming project mentioned earlier, I got a call from Keith Zellmer, a middle-aged farmer from Iowa with seven children. His family attended a small church with a very limited financial base. After several weeks in Albania, he sensed that this was where he was being called to serve, using his spiritual gifts and farming skills to help plant a church in a small village in Albania.

It seemed a long shot to me. We interacted along his journey. Against all odds, he and his family found the funding they needed, took the training required, and moved to Albania to play in the stadium that God called them to play in. Today, as I read their periodic missionary prayer letter and see images of a grown family and significant ministry impact in Albania, I am amazed by what God can do when we believe his calling and take the first steps in faith.

Dan (age forty-nine) was a pilot with United Airlines. His wife, Barrett, speaks several languages and has a professional career of her own. They had been married for seventeen years and have a lovely teenage daughter. Life was good. Dan's father and brothers are all pilots. They lived in the San Francisco Bay area, with all the trappings of our culture. Only they felt a longing for something more.

"We came to a point where I realized that we had climbed the ladder," Dan said, "but God was asking us if that ladder was leaning against his building or against our building."

Late one night, Dan began to explore the Internet for opportunities to serve around the world. As mission agencies responded, he became more and more excited about the adventure and the possibilities. He and his wife began to talk with friends about their desire to be used by God in the poorest parts of the world. Barrett felt surprised when her friends would ask her, "Why are you guys exploring this, Barrett? What are you missing here that you have to go so far away to find? You have everything here." When I last talked with Barrett, they were on their way to Colombia, South America, to serve in a school doing administrative work and operating a microenterprise program that creates work opportunities for graduating high school students. "It has been such a freeing experience," she said. "We simply have a new boss. We have just been traded from one team to another; we're using many of the same skills, only this time we have the ultimate coach."

Today they are adjusted to serving in South America and are having the time of their lives. It is a significant challenge—but also the adventure of their lives! Their friends, who at first considered them crazy, now see the vitality of their ministry and the new life and passion it has infused into their lives—and it doesn't seem quite so bizarre. In fact, for many of them, the choice of Dan and Barrett seems very refreshing.

There are probably ten "right" answers for you right now in your community and around the world, from a two-week investment all the way to a full-time opportunity, doing exactly what you were created to do in the place you are intended to be. Any one of those ten right answers would be a great place for you to start. Imagine the possibilities!

You, however, need to take the initiative to open the first doors and work in a servant-hearted but open-minded way with your church leadership. It is not a question of whether you will encounter obstacles; you will. Satan does not want you to finish reading this page, much less get out there and find a second-half serving opportunity. The *last* thing he wants is for someone with your talent to allocate part of his time toward expanding God's kingdom.

Ask your spouse and closest friends to pray for you as you decide which stadium you will play in: the marketplace, your church, your community, or somewhere around the world, or some combination of these. The question should not be if, but where.

Chapter 16

Finding Your Spot on the Team

Once you identify the right stadium, then what piece of work will you tackle? What model for serving will you create?

In my first ministry role, I created a niche that took advantage of my training and experience in marketing but required only about a third of my time and could be done mostly from home without significant travel. Finding this niche required creativity and negotiating with the organization, even though I would be volunteering my time.

It is up to each of us to do the hard work of understanding our own gifts and talents and then carving out a ministry or assignment that matches who we are and what God is calling us to.

Your Piece of Work

My best work always comes in creating, building, or influencing. Your best piece of work may be managing or systems or teaching. The role you play and the piece of work you choose will take into account your wiring, as defined in chapter eight. At this point you're looking for the specific assignment.

The most significant thing you can do to find this specific piece of work is to clearly define, in writing, who you are and what you are looking for. That way, organizations can present you with ministry assignments that fit you. The more vague you are about your skills and passions, the more difficult it will be to find your best match.

When Linda and I first moved to Charlotte from Canada, our real estate agent told us about Mecklenburg Community

Church. When we first visited, we felt surprised by the music, the casual atmosphere, the number of people in attendance, and the buzz factor about the relevance of the message. It was so different from what we were used to that we wondered if it was even legal to do church like that!

Then I made the "mistake" of attending a baptism service. My heart broke when I heard dozens of stories about people whose lives turned from darkness to light. We were hooked. How had this church reached these people? How had they created a place where so many totally unchurched folks would come and explore and find answers to their spiritual questions? I wondered if I could play even a small part in that adventure.

One sunny day in June, I had lunch with Jim White at a patio café. I felt glad to have an hour with the senior pastor because I really wanted to know what piece of work I should tackle. I ordered my favorite Reuben sandwich with fries (whoa, count the calories on that), and in his disciplined way, he had a dry turkey sandwich and unsweetened tea.

I asked Jim to describe the most compelling needs in the church. To my surprise, he responded by asking me, "If you could do anything in the world, what would it be?"

My heart flew back to the day I first saw Billy Graham on TV—probably a black-and-white set, with my brothers hanging around at someone else's house (since we didn't have a TV in our home). My mind felt drawn to that deep feeling in my stomach as I watched Dr. Graham preach. Right before my eyes, people were choosing to open their hearts to God. I remember sitting mesmerized on the floor, watching that program as they sang, "Just as I am without one plea." I could not turn my eyes away until the very last person came down the stadium stairs. I fought back the tears as I saw thousands of people bow their heads and give their lives to Jesus.

Something in me thrilled to see people move from darkness to light. Nothing else measured up. I realized that this is what caused me to get involved in foreign missions, because nowhere in our country did I see people coming to the Lord in droves.

So I was willing to go to Albania or wherever, if only I could be a part of seeing this happen. That is what caused me to turn my back on putting up new buildings, even though I loved creating those buildings. Imagine, I thought, *if every day I could be a part of this cosmic spiritual drama, working alongside the Spirit of God, to see people get up out of their chairs and choose life.*

As I looked off into the distance, thinking about Jim's question, I am sure he wondered if I was ever going to answer him. How could I put into words what I was dreaming? But it didn't take many words for Jim to get my drift. After all, Jim is a man who has given his entire life to the goal of seeing people come to the Lord. This church plant was designed to reach seekers. "What would you think about leading the evangelism effort here?" he asked. My reaction bubbled out into seven short words: "I could give my life to that."

So that's been my piece of work at Mecklenburg Community Church.

I've worked alongside each ministry of the church, helping them ensure that their strategy is intentionally designed to help those who wish to explore Christianity take one next step toward a relationship with God. I spend time training and coaching new Christians about how to gossip about their faith to unchurched friends. I lead discussion groups for spiritual seekers—something that I find so much fun that it should be illegal. Imagine spending each Monday night for six weeks with a group of eight to ten non-Christians who come because they want to explore the Christian faith. Imagine the thrill of seeing many of them cross the line of faith, right before your eyes.

I could just as easily use my skills to lead and grow the small group ministry, but that is not what interests me most. I could have accidentally ended up leading the middle school ministry. After all, many of my skills would be very useful there. But if you ever saw me trying to relate to kids at that stage of life, you would know how pathetic that would be. It's not my piece of work.

You can scan down a list of ministries in your own church, and see how your skills could apply in many of them. Finding the best piece of work for you is going to mean searching for where your heart engages and skills are needed.

There may be ten right answers to choose from, but the Bible doesn't give us a choice about getting in the game. If we don't find our piece of work, we run the risk of missing out on the greatest adventure of life. We run the risk of seeing everything we have built and invested in ending up in a landfill.

The Bible says that when God reviews our life one day in heaven, those things we did for ourselves or with impure motives will burn up as wood, hay, and stubble; but those works we did for God will last as gold, silver, and precious stones. We will earn an eternal reward for finding our piece of work and doing it for God's glory.

Personally, I'm going for the gold, silver, and precious stones.

Dr. Barry Sorrels is just an ordinary medical doctor, but he found an extraordinary piece of work that fits him to a tee. As a doctor who has practiced for decades, he knew that there is far more to running a successful practice than what they normally teach in medical school. At the same time, he has a passion to help doctors learn how to deal with faith issues in their practice. After all, God is the great healer.

In partnership with his church, he has created an adjunct curriculum offered to senior students at the University of Arkansas medical school. The program brings in leading experts in many nonmedical aspects of running a practice. The students have found it very helpful and the university couldn't be more pleased—but the privilege to open up discussions with graduating doctors regarding how and where faith comes into the science of medicine is priceless. Many students feel eager to talk openly and honestly about it, but had never found a safe forum. For Dr. Sorrels, it is a piece of work that fits him and his passions. And he is having the time of his life.

Tom McGehee developed a fascinating approach to collaborative work and problem solving, one that both large corporations and Christian nonprofit organizations find useful. When he felt a need to reorient his energy toward something eternal but was not at a spot to retire, he created another company, called WildWorks. WildWorks offers a unique collaborative work environment to corporations at normal marketplace fees so that he can offer the same service to churches and ministries for substantially reduced rates. This unique model enables him to pursue his second-half passions and build a business at the same time.

What would your own perfect assignment look like?

What would the environment be?

What kind of emotional or spiritual environments do you like the most?

What kinds of outcomes do you want to see from your work every day?

Your Serving Model

I love sailing. I love the wind in my hair. I love the silence when I shut off the engine, with only the sound of the waves and wind in my ears.

Sometimes I stop at a storefront window to admire beautiful wooden sailboat models. Their sleek, colorful hulls and white sails give me an immediate sense of freedom. In one brief moment, I can be transported from a bustling city street, with traffic noise and crowds marching by, to utter solitude out on a blue lake, with the boat heeled over at top racing speed.

What is it that makes a model so powerful? How can a two-foot-long sailboat model represent so much more than just a bunch of wood and fabric glued together?

Models like toy sailboats enable us to represent big things and big ideas in simple but useful ways. Some models we use for testing ideas without having to build the real thing. Architects make models of buildings so they can see what it might look like, ahead of time. Some statistical modeling is used to predict outcomes. Some models, such as sculpture, may not be intended to exactly replicate the original but to bring to mind certain feelings or ideas.[1]

Models of how others serve in their second half of life can provide you with a simplified way of comparing options and help you to experience in advance what it might be like.

Building Your Own Model

If you were building a sailboat model, you would need to decide ahead of time a few basic elements. Is it a single hull or catamaran? How many masts will it have? Will it be an historic replica or modern style? Beyond that, there will be endless small and subtle choices and modifications that you would add along the way to make it your unique model.

Assuming that you know the stadium you will be playing in for your second half, as well as the piece of work you want to do, then you have two big elements of your second-half serving model to decide:

1. *How much time will you work at your new calling?*

The broadest, most generic models would segment into four categories: reallocate part of your time; do stand-alone projects; take a full-time ministry role; or view the marketplace-as-ministry. You could say that the primary characteristic of your second-half serving model will be whether you choose to serve part of each week or month—say, ten hours a week, alongside of your normal work (or some revised version of that work)—or if you will tackle projects that require a significant concentration of effort over a period of time. Or maybe you are being called to leave what you do now and replace it with a completely new vocation. Others go through Halftime and are called to remain in their first-half career but with a dramatically different purpose and perspective. They feel called to serve in the marketplace, to bring light into a dark world.

2. *Will it need to be paid or unpaid?*

You need to determine if you will need to be paid or if you plan to volunteer your time.

Combining these two basic questions produces seven Half-time models:

part-time paid

part-time volunteer

paid projects

volunteer projects

full-time paid

full-time volunteer

full-time marketplace ministry

Thousands of creative ideas fit within those seven general categories. Consider the model Jim and Connie Phillips have constructed, and ask yourself what combination of time allocation and income generation best fits you.

It hit Jim one day while he watched a basketball game. "The game was between two Christian high school teams," Jim said, "and I found myself thinking, My faith is a spectator sport; I watch it more than I live it." Jim's life was full of good things, but he felt restless. Life had become a wash of "sameness": common routines, learned patterns, repetitive structure. He made a good living as a successful accountant, had a wonderful family, and was involved in his church. But he sensed that he lacked the most important thing: life-giving passion.

He went home and told his wife, Connie, his thoughts. He thought it was time to step off the sidelines and into the painful reality of the world. They would have to do something intentional. But what?

After much soul-searching, they felt God leading them to pull their kids from Christian schools and enroll them in a public school system struggling under mounting problems. Then they would get involved in that school as parents and look for opportunities to serve.

Although they would choose the best possible public school for their children, they knew they were gambling on faith. Both of them knew that their lives would never be the same. Moving the family out of its carefully crafted comfort zone would invite feelings of loneliness, fear, isolation, and hurt.

When Connie went to pick up her four children after their first day of public school, she got her first taste of the family's new reality. She found them huddled together and alone on a bench in front of school. They were beginning to understand the cost of their parents' decision to reach the world with God's love and the cross you must sometimes bear.

The Phillips' journey of courageous faith had begun. They knew the stadium they were playing in, and they had just found the piece of work they were called to. But what model? How would it fit into their existing life?

Eventually they found themselves paired with another couple from church, Larry and Ann McCraw. Because of each couple's growing public school experience, they saw the need not only for mentoring but also for sexual abstinence teaching. So together they formed a small group at church with this ministry in mind. In time they developed and taught a sexual abstinence and mentoring program called Excel, a program that they have now used in nearly all the public junior high schools in their district. Through the efforts of their small group, they recently received federal funding that allowed them to hire a program director and two part-time employees.

The model for Jim and Connie began as a "volunteer project" but has blossomed into a full-blown ministry. Jim still does it (part-time volunteer) alongside his CPA practice; it has become Connie's primary vocation (full-time volunteer).

Today, thirteen public schools in their county welcome them with open arms. More than 3,500 students are now involved with Excel, as well as 700 adult volunteers. "One of the most exciting things has been seeing God raise up sixty-five local churches that have stepped in and contributed time and resources for their particular area schools," Connie says. "That's a key to success."

Jim and Connie Phillips are no longer in the stands with a spectator kind of faith. They found their piece of work, a model that works for them, and are fully deployed with a faith that not only has broken a sweat, but is filled with the life-giving passion Jim once only dreamed about.[2]

How Will You Serve?

Do you love to tackle projects that have a beginning and an end and work intensely until they are completed? Do you prefer this over having an ongoing job description?

Do you envision a ten-hour-a-week formal staff role for an established organization?

Will you be a periodic consultant, bringing specialized skills to multiple organizations?

Do you feel called to leave your present career entirely to launch into something completely different, full time?

PART III

IMPORTANT MIDLIFE ISSUES I NEVER DREAMED OF

Chapter 17

A Completely Quiet Locker Room:
Doing It Alone, the Wrong Way

I moved through the Halftime journey on my own, largely in isolation from my wife and other close friends who could have counseled, advised, and supported me. With one exception: I spoke openly with Andrew Mitton, my business partner. Even then, I found it difficult to talk openly with another guy about the deepest inner longings of my heart.

Still, Andrew helped me with tactical issues. He helped me assess my financial situation and plan our family's funding for the medium term. He helped by providing a sounding board as I experimented with serving opportunities. We mostly talked about all this from a pragmatic viewpoint, with little attention to the emotional or spiritual side of the process.

But remember, Halftime is about coming to understand our longings for significance, our passions and God's call, then discovering a plan to put all of these together. I needed to learn how to communicate on a deeper level if I were to include others and their insights into my journey.

As I began to test out projects and potential serving roles, I missed the valuable insights of Linda and close male friends that could have helped me debrief. Their insights would have helped me to better assess how and where I could best contribute.

I simply did not include Linda in the process as much as I should have. We talked about what I wanted to do, about what I wanted my life to be about. We worked closely on the five-year plan and strategy to make this transition. She even came with me to visit the international mission organization I first worked with, and we talked about each of my initial forays into ministry and what worked and what did not. So, if she was involved at each of these points, why do I say that I did not include her in the process as much as I should have?

She was along for the ride, but it could have been a much deeper, richer, shared journey. First and foremost, I confess I did not equally concern myself with her interest, her unique God-given design, nor in pursuing what this might look like for her in this second-half adventure. I did not communicate with her how I felt along the way but only what I was "thinking." She knew the strategy and tactical elements of my Halftime journey—but Halftime is a soul journey. I did not let her into much of my soul's journey. I simply didn't operate in that space. Explaining how I felt about something seemed like a waste of time. Emotions had proven so unreliable in my career and everyday problem solving that I relegated them to the anecdotal category.

Because I did not effectively communicate at this depth and had not opened the door to deep dialogue with a few close friends or with Linda, I did not interact with anyone about heart issues. I did not discuss how closely my identity was wrapped up in being a successful real estate developer. I did not tell her that I was at a loss to know how to find a new identity. I did not mention my fear of failing in this new ministry arena. I did not reveal my skepticism about my ability to juggle work, family, marriage, and increased ministry. I did not ask out loud, "Why am I so driven to accomplishment? Do I have a distorted under-lying view of my value before God?"

At times I wondered if I were going crazy by thinking the way I did. Here God had given me the passion and skill to develop real estate—so why did I not feel content to just pursue that with all my strength? I didn't talk with Linda or anyone about these feelings, however. I should have, and so should you. The bottom line is, I attempted to do Halftime alone, sorting between selfish or unrealistic ambitions and real promptings of

God without the insights of those who knew me and loved me the most. Crazy! Don't do it.

I have to mention another important benefit of doing Halftime in close community with a few others: you will deepen and strengthen those relationships in the journey, and they will prove very important to your longevity in your second half. Foremost in this crowd of supporters is your spouse. One of the most significant things many men discover in the second half is the value of deep relationships. Today, I rank relationships at the very top of the list of my assets. Fifteen years ago, they weren't even on the radar screen.

For example, when I consider a new ministry opportunity these days, I ask at least three key questions:

1. Do I really enjoy doing ministry with these people?
2. Is this in my area of greatest giftedness?
3. Will it make a significant impact?

Notice that relationships come at the front end of all these questions. And I ask them regularly.

Including a Few Close Friends

By including your spouse and a few close, same-gender friends in this Halftime journey, your relationships will get woven that much closer together.

John Leffin lives in Wisconsin. For his entire career, he has worked for a major consulting firm. He has traveled a lot, serving clients around the world. At age forty-four, he and his wife have the typical family issues, with two girls in their teens and an active church and social life. Summers are packed with tennis, golf, and having friends and family to the cottage in northern Wisconsin. The school year is filled with sports, musicals, small group Bible study, and helping kids with school work. At the same time, John works at staying in shape, growing his personal spiritual life, and investing in his relationship with his wife.

After twenty-one years in the consulting business, John found that he had some options regarding where he took his career and how he invested some of his time and talents for the second half. Up to that point, John's story probably echoes many of us in Halftime. But what makes John's story different is how he engaged others in the journey with him.

At times he felt disillusioned, even disoriented, in the process. In those times he had people to turn to and had cultivated an openhearted way of communicating with them.

John's team consisted of his family, close friends, men in his Bible study group, his financial advisor, pastors at his church, and current and former colleagues. Opening up to and engaging this many people was a stretch for him and not a typical "guy thing." He had to be willing to share from his heart and soul and be ready to have his thinking challenged. Most team members encouraged him in the journey, while a few had trouble understanding what he was doing. In the end, the encouragement and support gave John the intestinal fortitude to make a major career and life change, with little clarity as to what lay ahead.

As part of this journey, John needed someone who could directly relate to what he was going through. He found this in one of his partners, Jeff Beech. Jeff had started his Halftime journey about a year earlier and provided invaluable insights, ideas, experiences, and support. They had similar careers and second-half goals. Jeff could relate to John's experience and helped give him the courage to make a change.

Finding a trusted coach through this process can often mean the difference between thinking about second-half goals and actually achieving them. Find a coach at *www.halftime.org.*

Now that John has jumped headfirst into Halftime, his team has provided ongoing encouragement and support. Let's face it, we all go through buyer's remorse at times and need someone to assure us that we made the right decision. Without this support, it is easy to say, "Well, I tried this Halftime thing for a while, but I think I'll go back to what I know best and feels most comfortable to me." A team like John's can be invaluable during the Halftime transition.

Men and Women Tend to Be Different in This Area

Elements of the Halftime journey can be dramatically different for men and women. First, many women in Halftime already are very much in touch with their emotions regarding midlife and can effectively communicate those feelings. Further, they are more likely to have close, intimate friends with whom they can regularly discuss their feelings and aspirations. This simply is not true of most men.

I usually have lunch a couple times a week with different individuals who have just begun the Halftime journey. Each month I spend time with rooms full of these people, all across the country. I am always intentional in the conversation to get around to asking them, "Tell me about your friends." That is a simple but stunning question for most men. Their response normally goes something like this: "I have some close friends at work ... well, actually they are business associates, and we almost never talk about anything but business, cars, and stuff. However, there are some guys at church ... well, I really don't see them often with my travel, but we have had some deeper conversations during annual men's retreat. There is a neighbor; we're kind of buds, but he is on a completely different wavelength when it comes to what matters in life. You know, I really don't have any close friends."

Most men in America have no close, intimate male friends. Be honest; do you? I mean, close friends who already have permission to challenge you in the most sensitive areas of your life. Friends with whom you have had many open discussions about your inner world.

Women, on the other hand, normally answer that they have three or more close friends, and they explain how they have become soul mates on one wavelength or another. They talk at length about life and what they are feeling along the way. So, from my experience, women who find themselves in Halftime are far ahead of men in terms of doing the journey with others—with one caveat. They seldom confront each other. For these relationships to provide us with the real feedback and insight we need, we must hear the straight truth from our friends. Our friends need to be willing to problem solve with us.

Today, I have these kinds of relationships. I have learned how to put my feelings into words and openly dialogue with a few close friends about them. These guys are very willing to tell me straight up what they see. They provide very specific, practical ideas for solutions to the issues or weaknesses I face.

Jack Willome, an executive with a major home builder in his city, found himself bored and frustrated with his work. An advisor listened to his story and said that, from his perspective, Jack's boredom came because he is a problem solver by nature and he had already solved most of the major problems in his organization. He would either have to move to a larger organization with new and bigger challenges or find a new area of passion to invest in and renegotiate how much time he spent with his present employer.

Jack could not imagine either of those things happening.

Only weeks later, Jack got a call from the mayor of his city, asking him to help solve a major water problem in the community. Much to his surprise, his company offered him work flexibility, thus launching his second-half adventure. Today he is involved in multiple ministry ventures and is making a big difference. Jack included other men in this journey—something unusual for most of us. In my view, in this area of including others, Jack's second-half story provides an outstanding example.

Jack knows that he will always have blind spots that his friends can help him discover, and imbalances that they can help him correct. As he says, "When I've gotten myself overcommitted and overloaded, it's been because I've been tempted to say yes to opportunities that appeal to my ego and my pride."

Jack gathered some of his closest friends together and asked them to hold him accountable for how he invested his resources. They have been friends for many years, and he knows that "it is just as important to them as it is to me that the gifts that God has given me be used for his purposes."

They form a kind of personal board of directors to whom he has given permission to challenge him and ultimately approve every new project or major assignment he takes on. "Because of my inability to discern what I should say yes and no to, they have final approval for any new projects I take on," he explains. "I need these men in my life. They hold me to task as to how I use my time. Periodically they come in and ask to see my calendar, to see if I am spending enough time with my family, or too much time away from home. When I am being deceived they can see it, so they protect me. This is how Jesus worked. He worked closely with just twelve men, and then within that he had a core of three men—Peter, James, and John—that he did life most intimately with."

Connecting with Your Spouse

Your spouse cannot provide all the input you need at Halftime. But he or she understands you in a very unique way, and you need that input. More importantly, the second half of life provides an opportunity to think intentionally about what your life together could be like. If finding significance in your second half comes only through giving yourself away, then you need to begin with your spouse. How will you intentionally give of your best resources to enable your spouse to reach his or her dreams and goals? How will you engage your spouse in your journey in a way that honors and values him or her? This can be a scary process for both people.

Dr. Terry Taylor rose to the top of the Navigators, a large national ministry that focuses on discipleship. He spent fifteen exciting, all-consuming years as the CEO performing at what seemed like the peak of his game. But now in his sixties, after passing the baton on to a new leader, he has had a chance to pause and think about where to go from here. He realized that in his early second-half years, from forty-five to sixty—when he had so much fun—he had neglected to really understand his wife's second-half dreams and aspirations.

My son, Carter (now age sixteen), and I traveled to Colorado to ski, and we had a chance to spend several hours with Dr. Taylor. I had watched his life from a distance and already knew he was the kind of man I would like to be at age sixty. I wanted my son to have the privilege of listening to him. It was invaluable for Carter and me to hear Terry say that if he had it to do over again, he would have paused long before now to really understand his wife and her skills and help her find the space where she could really flourish.

Terry and his wife have since helped hundreds of other couples plan their second half with greater clarity and unity. As Carter and I left his office, we both felt as if we had seen inside the heart of a man who walks with God and loves his wife deeply and felt confident enough to describe his secret longing that he had been more mindful of his wife's needs. Terry told us that his greatest thrill today is seeing his wife flourish in the place where she ministers to other couples who want to do their second half together.

Wrestling with God

Most of all, you need to wrestle with God in Halftime. Ultimately, he is the one who will call the shots in your life. He speaks into your Halftime journey through the Bible, prayer and meditation, other people, and circumstances.

What does it look like to wrestle with God on a heart level at Halftime?

Nelson Malwitz manages research and development for Sealed Air Corporation, a major player in the bubble wrap market. He is not a senior executive in the classic sense of the word, but his scientific abilities and thought leadership have helped push his firm to the front of the innovation curve. He holds thirteen patents for products and processes he invented. His wife, Marguerite, is an artist. They have two boys just finishing college. They live in Connecticut and love to ski in Vermont, where they have a cottage. Nelson calls himself "an expert at being the quint-essential baby boomer."

He has moved through Halftime and today spends half his time in corporate America and half his time leading a ministry called the Finishers Project. Finishers has catalyzed change in many leading mission agencies and been part of moving more than five hundred people into missions at midlife. If you met Nelson, you would not suspect that God would use a normal guy like him to launch a movement of that magnitude. If you casually assessed Nelson's presentation style or humble, self-deprecating demeanor, you probably would not see that he daily wrestles with God in his Halftime journey.

One of Nelson's classic lines is "God asks us to present our bodies at midlife as a living sacrifice. That's countercultural. It's almost un-American. But it's the bottom line."

Wow. That comes from somewhere deep. And when you stop and think about it, it really is the bottom line for a significant second half: presenting our bodies to God as a living sacrifice and wrestling with him personally in this journey, asking him to use our lives for the greatest impact, to his honor and glory. If I were honest, I would have to say that I am not sure I'm really ready to do that.

Nelson began his Halftime journey while serving as an elder at his church. In that context he spent enough time with men a few years ahead of him to see modeled what other guys were doing in their second half. In some cases he felt impressed; in other cases he felt turned off. He walked alongside these men, seeking their input. Nelson is not a man who easily shares his feelings, but he is way out in front of the pack in his commitment to wrestle daily with the Lord. His view is simple: "The Lord is the general manager who really puts you to work."

After wrestling with God to discover his assignment, Nelson negotiated a fifty-fifty time split with Sealed Air Corporation. That allowed him to keep one foot in the marketplace and keep some income coming in, while his nest egg grew and allowed him to launch this ministry. He found that when he cut back his role at work, he no longer had as many people reporting to him, which opened up a ton of emotional margin—a big surprise. In addition, the 50 percent of the work he retained was all in his area of strength, and as a result he can do it without having to really stretch. These combined factors have made this model of serving a win for both the company and Nelson's new ministry.

Even after making this transition, Nelson still gets up each morning, pours a cup of coffee, and opens his Bible to begin his day, wrestling with God. Once, while he was in Halftime, he came to a chapter in Exodus where the Lord says that he wanted only willing workers to build the tabernacle and that he expected them to deliver their very best. Nelson asked God to make him content to bring his best effort to God each day and willingly offer it back to the Lord. Some time later, he came to a chapter on tithing. As he wrestled with God, he realized that tithing has to do with time, talent, and treasure—that the Lord asks us to give our first fruits. When the harvest comes, we are not even to eat until we have given our tithe. Again he opened the door for the Lord to make that idea a vital part of his life, and today it is.

I asked Nelson to explain to me his focus on wrestling with God through his Halftime journey. "Unless you are willing to spend time with the Lord," he said, "you will not find your assignment—because ultimately it comes from him. It requires eye contact with the General Manager. The reason is that the Lord is far more interested in our righteousness than in our results."

The most healthy and productive Halftime journey happens with others, locally, over time. It requires a willingness to dig deep into the soul to put our finger on the real issues and then to welcome our spouse, a few intimate same-gender friends, and the Lord into the process.

But how on earth do you do that? Let's take a look.

Chapter 18

Doing Halftime with Others

Bob Buford has discovered that the most successful Halftime transitions happen *with others, locally, over time.*

When you stop and think about it, it's a no-brainer. After all, long ago God said, "Two are better off than one, because together they can work more effectively. If one of them falls down, the other can help him up. . . . Two people can resist an attack that would defeat one person alone. A rope made of three cords is hard to break" (Ecclesiastes 4:9–10, 12 TEV).

I think I know what you're thinking. If you were to write out what is on your mind right now, I bet it would include some of the following thoughts: "How do I specifically include others in my Halftime journey? Where do you find these people? What role can my spouse play in this process? Aren't some things unrealistic to expect her/him to provide? Why is 'locally' such a big factor? And about the 'over time' idea ... you need to know that when I make up my mind to make a change in my life, I get on with it. I make it happen—like *now.* So why poke along 'over time' through a methodical process?" Great questions, and we're going to tackle them.

If these are the three big factors that Bob Buford has found to be critical to midlife transition, then let's walk through how you really do it, starting with the hardest step for many of us: *Tell your spouse you need some help.*

Now, that's a scary thought. I was sitting across from Cindy and Rick at one of my favorite Mexican food places. We met Rick earlier in chapter 14. He is a financial planner who wants to get involved in a compassionate care ministry. For more than a year, Rick and I had been talking about his unsettledness at midlife. He had worked through the major issues and was coming to the conclusion that he should ratchet down his role at the investment firm and create just enough space to lead an effort that served the poor in our community. We met for lunch so that I could make sure he and Cindy were on the same wavelength and to surface any feelings that Cindy might have.

I opened our time together by saying something like, "Cindy, I wanted to get your reactions to what Rick and I have been talking about the past year; about his feelings that he was not having the kind of impact he would like. He senses that he spends too much of his time managing investments, which for the most part roll up and down with the major market swings. It's caused him to pause and reflect on what he really cares about and how to retool life so he can invest some of his time in the areas of his passion—"

I got just that far when Cindy turned, looked Rick right in the eye, and asked, "Rick, honey, is that really how you feel?" It was apparent that she had no idea he was feeling this way.

He looked obviously relieved that I had put into words what he was feeling but simply had had a hard time communicating to Cindy. I knew exactly how he felt. I'd been there myself.

Most men can relate to Rick. Some women, as well. What on earth makes it so hard for us to explain these feelings to our spouse right from the start? My guess is that fear is the biggest hurdle. I feared that Linda would not understand me, that she would think I was simply discontent with a "normal" life of working hard at my career, spending time with my family, and living happily-ever-after. There's also a fear of rejection. We fear that, if we've been a strong provider, our spouse will view us as something less now that she will not feel as attracted to the person we want to be in our second half.

Second, we need to sort through our thoughts and find words that match them. For some of us, that takes time.

If you feel like Rick, I have a recommendation for you. Go somewhere to be alone for a couple hours, somewhere relaxing where you won't be interrupted. Take a large Hallmark-type card with you—one with lots of blank space in it—and write a note to your spouse that says something like the following:

Dear _____,

I am surprised to find myself at midlife. I can hardly imagine that I am about halfway through. I want the second half of our life to really count for something significant. I first realized this when I began to feel [write in some of the feelings that first started your Halftime journey and some of your most recent feelings].

I know this will be a journey and will involve change for both of us, but I want our second half to be something we plan together. As we process things, I believe I will need your very best thoughts and ideas about [list the kinds of issues you feel you will want her or his thoughts and ideas on].

There will be times I feel confused, times I don't understand how I am feeling. I need you to be patient but also to persist at asking me thoughtful questions that will help me think through these important life issues from a different perspective—and one that includes the best for both of us in this journey.

If I had taken a risk and given Linda a card like that at the beginning of my Halftime journey, it would have done three important things:

1. It would have helped her feel more secure to explore the possibilities with me regarding our future. Many spouses actually hinder their partner's Halftime journey, because they do not understand what drives it or where it is going. So they instinctively look for every way to put on the brakes. As they begin to rein in their spouse, it even further exasperates their feeling of being confined with midlife responsibilities. You can proactively manage this phenomenon by explaining what is driving your Halftime feelings and that you want to experience the journey together.

2. A card like this would have encouraged Linda to become an active participant in our midlife transition. It would have made it easier for her to remain engaged in the journey, even during times when I found it hard to communicate what was going on down deep inside me. From time to time, I still would have needed to get away to my "cave" to process things; but the door would always have remained open for her to pursue my inner thoughts.

3. Most importantly, this would have put the topic on the table early and would have eliminated the risk of me working partway through the journey on my own until I could clearly communicate my thoughts. If you wait until that point to raise the subject, your spouse will feel as though he or she has been intentionally left out of the loop and is expected to move forward with little, if any, ownership in the future.

One last thing. I suggest that you tear these pages out of this book, so that your spouse doesn't read it and you lose all the credit for having the insight to write her such a great card!

If you know of another couple that has already gone through a Halftime transition, consider connecting with them as a couple and encourage your spouse to interact with the respective spouse about this transition.

Remember that what you do significantly affects your spouse. I had no idea that my role as a real estate developer provided a context for my wife to communicate about our family to her friends and in our community. My transition drastically affected our financial security, which matters a great deal to Linda. This is not just another business deal; it is about planning your lives together, intentionally working alongside each other on some parts and separately on some other parts.

Your second half provides an opportunity to celebrate your spouse in new ways and to focus on what it will take for him or her to flourish.

For John and Loretta Leffin, my consultant friend from the last chapter, Halftime provided a return to what they experienced early in their marriage: adventure, togetherness, and a sense of possibility. While Loretta felt a bit nervous about John's midlife restlessness, the process they followed became a time of renewal, with new dreams and possibilities.

"For several years, our lives were running pretty smoothly on autopilot," Loretta said. "John was busy as a partner in his consulting firm, and I was balancing my time as a volunteer and worship leader at church. At the center of all of this was our role as parents to our teenage daughters, Melissa and Krista. Life was good and pretty predictable. Staying the course was a comfortable and fairly low risk alternative to the next several years."

So why make a change? As their faith grew, John and Loretta both knew that God had other plans for their second half. Initially, Loretta served as John's primary sounding board, helping him think through all the implications of making a major career and life change. The challenge was having the willingness and patience to listen, and the courage to act on what they heard.

Before they could act, they needed to consider a number of important questions. What would be the financial impact of this change, near and long term? What would the impact be on their household if John had more time available at home? What would this mean to his identity that for years centered on being a partner in a premier consulting firm? How strong was his faith, really?

As you know, John surrounded himself with a strong team to go through this journey with him. Loretta served as the team captain. As on any team, you look to the captain for guidance, leadership, and moral support. Captains steady the team and don't lose their cool when the game is on the line. They give great pep talks at Halftime. They challenge you when you want to take the easy way out. They pick you up when you feel down. And finally, they stand at the center of the celebration at the end of each big win.

By carefully including your spouse on your Halftime team, you can turn an unsettling experience into an opportunity for your relationship to grow to an even deeper level.

Finding Those Friends

When someone asks me for help in Halftime, I often advise them to find some friends. Real friends. That may seem odd, but it is not easy to find two or three others at the same stage of life as you are, with whom you share a certain chemistry and who will invest the time to build a deep friendship. They are few and far between. The good news is, however, those guys know they need friendships too. It's up to you to take the initiative.

What kind of people are you looking for? In my experience, they need to have at least the following characteristics:

- You just like hanging out together.
- Same stage of life, so that they can relate to the issues you face.
- Same gender, since you will be sharing very personal information. The risk is simply too high to do this with someone of the opposite gender to whom you are not married.
- Spiritually mature. You want this person to provide godly wisdom for your life—and that can come only from a godly life.

Where Can You Find These Friends?
Old friends

You have some old friends, or perhaps a sibling or cousin, who has been a part of your life since you were a kid. Chances are that they face similar issues. Maybe he is a long-time colleague who started at the company when you did as a trainee more than twenty years ago, and he too faces the possibility of early retirement. Such people tend to live at a distance now since we move all over the country during our first half of life. Because you have so much history with them, however, inviting them to talk regularly by phone and to meet periodically is an approach worth taking.

My cousin, Keith Dodds, lives in Canada. He's a year younger than I am, and we've been friends since I can remember.

(Now that I think about it, the fact that he is a year younger used to mean a lot when I was ten and he was nine.) All the history we share means that we can talk shorthand. I don't need to qualify what I say because he knows my heart and underlying motives. My life has a track record of success and of good leadership, but none of that wows him. I have a track record of following God, but he knows my blind spots and has permission to ask tough questions. My family, like all families, has a history of certain weaknesses, and I've noticed that he watches for signs of them emerging in my life, with the goal of helping me see them before they become issues. Each time I develop a set of five-year goals, I get his input. It has proven invaluable.

We meet at least once a year to spend a few days together. This summer, Keith and I took our families to the Canadian Rockies. Between outings of extreme mountain biking, swimming, and hiking, we had time to download the latest in each other's life and then provide perspective and real advice. The value of having someone with this kind of tenure, speaking into your life, is that they have a deeper context from which to view issues. On the other hand, sometimes they are too anchored by your past to provide optimal counsel for the changes you want to make (or desire for God to make) in your future.

Find Peers at Church

Church at its core is a community of people pursuing God together and making an impact on their world. No better Halftime partners can be found than those willing to pursue God with you as you change your community for the better together.

One aspect of my pastoral role at Mecklenburg Community Church is leading the Halftime ministry. We gather together people at midlife and cast a vision for the idea of moving from success to significance. This provides the opportunity for them to connect with each other. Small groups form naturally as people begin to share their lives and journey. If no such service is available in your church, consider being a catalyst to bring your peers together. (For church resources go to *www.successtosignificance.com*.)

Find Peers in the Marketplace

You can also find these kinds of friendships through peer networking among business or professional people in your community. Perhaps you know a doctor who from time to time works in the OR with you who is a Christian and at the same stage of life. Invite him to do whatever you do for recreation and begin to ask him if he has ever had midlife thoughts similar to the ones you are having.

Be intentional

Whether you ask old friends, peers from the business community, or build a Halftime small group at your church, be intentional about finding people who can serve in this role. Look for people with whom you enjoy spending time, who are not intimidated by you in any way. If you are a person of faith, it is important that they draw their wisdom from the Word of God and follow him. Most importantly, they need to be willing to create the time to meet with you regularly.

Give them the big idea of the transition you want to make in life. Provide them with some reading material so that they can become familiar with the idea of Halftime and redefining success as significance.

Plan to meet with these friends regularly to talk about your latest thoughts and feelings as you begin your journey. You may need to meet weekly at the start, and then monthly or quarterly thereafter. Over time, their input will become less abstract and more specific as you begin to test ministry opportunities and debrief those experiences together.

It is up to you to take the initiative to schedule your meetings and find places that feel relaxed but convenient for them.

Bring a list of issues and topics for which you want their input, but leave the agenda open enough that they can take it a different direction if they want to explore something else that may have escaped your notice.

Act on what they tell you. Obviously, not every idea they have will be a good one, but when they present a good idea, put it into play right away and communicate with them that you have put it into play. It is important for a friend making this level of investment in you to see you take it seriously and know that they are making a difference.

I am fortunate to have some close guy friends, but it did not just happen by accident; it was intentional. These relationships are critical if I am going to stay in the game for the long haul and do it in a healthy way. Bottom line is, I need them, which is a hard thing to admit in writing.

You already know Randy, my closest friend. I introduced him in chapter 9 and the tension he faces, trying to create margin and time for reflection. With four kids, a commitment to a great marriage, and crazy work hours as a doctor, you would think the last thing he has time for is a friendship. Wrong! I'm not sure why Randy is so far out in front of the pack of most of us men in the area of relationships, but I'm guessing it's a combination of personality type and a wonderful mother who invested hundreds of hours teaching him how to communicate his real feelings. By walking alongside Randy for the past six years, I have learned a tremendous amount about how this kind of Halftime peer interaction really works.

Randy was the anesthesiologist in the operating room when our oldest girl, Carrie, had an operation. Later we spotted him in the church lobby and introduced ourselves. We invited his family to join our weekly small group Bible study with five other couples and a total of nineteen kids (go figure). He felt drawn to how my faith really changed how I lived, how I spent my time and money. As we began to build a friendship, I wondered if I could help him in his effort to integrate his faith into family life. Little did I know how much I would learn from him!

Sometimes Randy would call with no real purpose, just to catch up. I will never forget the first time I realized toward the end of the call that he had called with no agenda: there was nothing he needed from me, he was not arranging for anything. He called just to chat. I wasn't sure if someone could *do* that. *You can't just pick up the phone and call someone for no apparent reason except just to talk,* I thought. It sure seemed awkward to me. To my knowledge, I had never thought of doing such a thing, much less actually had the nerve to do it. At that point I realized I had a lot to learn from Randy about being a real friend.

Today, six years later, he has called me every week without fail, despite an often hectic schedule. Why? Because it matters to him. We work out together, play tennis together, and hang out on the weekend together. Most of all, we simply do life together, and in so doing we give each other the priceless gift of a peer's perspective. We take the relational risk of speaking the truth in love.

We challenge, encourage, inform, and admonish one another. We call on each other when severely tempted, ask for help when we get in over our head, explain complex situations that need to be untangled confidentially.

A year ago, I got an email from Randy that set me on my heels. As you read the following note, think about how valuable this kind of insight will be to your Halftime journey—and think about who would risk your friendship to tell you something this straight.

> Lloyd,
>
> *For some reason I was thinking about you and Carter.*
>
> *He reminds me of my teen days that seem like yesterday. I know these can be challenging times, but thank God, he's a good kid with a heart for what's right. I wanted to share a couple of abbreviated thoughts that may be totally off base, so take them for whatever they may or may not provide.*
>
> *As we've discussed before, he's dealing with that "not living up to dad's expectations" thing. I think, however, at this age it begins to evolve into a "I've not become what my dad wanted" thing. Soon to become a "I've not become what I wanted (or should be)" thing. He will rebel or get angry seemingly toward your*

perceived expectations, but he is really beginning to own it as "self" and will deep down get angry or struggle there.

Well, enough with the psycho-babble. The bottom line of my possibly-off-base thought is this: what he needs more than anything now is your relationship, respect and approval. Much of his course, pertaining to you steering the boat, anyway, has been set and your specific direction will increasingly lose bang for the buck. Your relationship—the depth, that is—will pay much higher dividends.

Hope this carries some meaning.

Your Friend,

Randy Williams

Allow me to unpack this email for you. Randy thought that I needed to change how I go about helping my son become all that God intends for him to be. That was hard to hear, but a very important message, and I began to make that change right away. It's not that Carter is underachieving. He's a really great guy, and I am so proud of him. He has lots of friends, knows how to be a real friend, which I didn't learn until later in life, is on the high school track and swim team, gets A's and B's, and is responsible with money. But he's not driven like I was.

But what lies between the lines is equally as important.

- Notice that Randy is involved enough in my life to observe Carter and see this need for change.
- He took time out of his day to think about where I need to grow.
- He and I are headed in the same direction, so his input helps me move to where I want to go. An important part of living a significant second half is leaving a spiritual legacy through our children and grandchildren.
- He took a risk, couched in love, to communicate directly what he saw, yet all the while recognizing that he might not have the whole perspective.

That is the kind of input you and I both need at midlife. The subject for you may not concern how you need to change your style of relating with your teenage son, but rather about managing your spending or time with God or controlling your thought life.

The benefits of doing Halftime with others cannot be overstated. I have experienced what it is like to be alone with very little input from others, and I have since experienced what it is like to walk through the journey with others and God. From my experience, you want to invest in finding these kinds of peers and nurturing these relationships.

Last, as you make this journey, remember that you are attempting something countercultural. Your friends and business colleagues are watching. Perhaps one of the most significant impacts of your second half will be the impact you have on those who know and respect you from your first half as they watch you go through the process.

Your Next Step

Which old friends could help you in Halftime?

Who do you like hanging around with who is also in midlife?

Where are you most likely to connect with peers who are spiritually mature and wrestling with midlife issues?

Chapter 19

Tackled from Behind by the Culture Gap

If you are not careful, an unseen opponent will tackle you from behind, just as you head for the end zone with the ball in your hands. That opponent is the vast culture gap between your marketplace experience and leading in a nonprofit organization. Even with the insights of close trusted peers, you can expect to experience a sense that you have entered another world.

I can almost guarantee that you are thinking: *Come on, how big an issue can that be?* After all, the people you'll be working with are normal people. People just like you who live in subdivisions like yours and shop at the same mall where you shop. How much different can their work culture be?

Trust me. They are *very* different.

My own experience was so counter-intuitive. The very first role I played in the nonprofit world was with a cross-cultural mission organization, whose entire focus was understanding and serving people in other cultures. They specialize in cross-cultural communication, and yet because I spoke the same language, wore the same clothes and visited the same restaurants they did, we failed to see that I was as cross-cultural to that organization as if I came from another country.

My first day in the office surprised me. I expected people to arrive early, stay late, and feel excited about the opportunity they had to make a significant impact around the world. Instead, it seemed to me that some simply went through the motions.

I found people who were not a good match for their jobs and as a result were under performing. They remained in those roles because the sense of community did not enable the leadership to hold people accountable to a higher level of performance. Leadership did not feel free to move people out when they no longer fit the role.

From a driven, businessperson's perspective, the office seemed strangely quiet at 4:30 p.m. as people filed out, leaving me wondering if they were there because they considered this their calling or if it had inadvertently become just a job.

I compared their apparent lack of urgency with the intense level of urgency in our real estate development business. Where was the drive I saw in the marketplace?

I had been given the assignment to create a more comprehensive marketing strategy. As I explained my proposed new strategy to the leadership team, I could see that my language made them feel uncomfortable. When I spoke of "customers" and "market segmentation," it sounded so secular, cold, and mercenary to them. So they wondered if I had a cold heart toward the people they were trying to serve. But for me? It was my native language.

If leadership is influence, then it became clear to me within the first year that the tools I used in the marketplace to lead and influence were not working in this culture. I led in the marketplace with better ideas, energy, enthusiasm, and capital. These people knew I had been effective, but before they would follow my lead or implement my strategies, they wanted to know if I really cared about their cause. Did I have an informed worldview? They wondered if I really cared about the people around the world whom they were committed to helping. Did I understand the mission, or was I just another type-A business guy, out to prove something to God or to feel good about himself?

These are good people, committed to God and to his global cause. In my view, they are the heroes of the faith. They work in this ministry because they believe strongly in the cause. They are paid less than market value, and on top of that, many of them raised funds for their own salary. Go figure. As a result, they feel something like a volunteer or free agent. Leading people who are essentially volunteers is dramatically different than leading a team of paid architects, builders, and subcontractors which I am used to.

Neither the organization nor I were prepared for the vast culture gap between our two worlds. From leadership strategies, to the philosophical differences about measuring results in a nonprofit environment, to even the basic business language I used, we lived worlds apart. These cultural differences could easily have derailed my Halftime transition. For many, it has.

The more informed you become about the culture gap between the business-and-professional world and the ministry-or-nonprofit world, the healthier your transition will be.

Every year, the international mission organization I have worked with gathers key leaders for an annual planning retreat. It's an offsite event in a remote camp setting, designed to be a place where the general director can cast a vision for where the organization needs to go, and then the major departments can begin to plan what it will take to reach that vision and ultimately to bring those diverse plans into a coordinated effort. Sounds reasonable. My first year with the organization, I thought I would be able to really contribute in this strategic planning area.

Little did I know.

Part of the way through that first annual planning retreat, I realized that many of the people there had never studied strategic planning or done it in a corporate setting. People held vastly different mental images of the purpose of the retreat and they had dramatically different views on the theology of planning. Some believed that since they were operating in God's arena, it might be okay to lay out some good general ideas about what to do in the coming year, but that ultimately it was up to God to make it happen.

It was an ah-ha moment in my nonprofit-world planning experience when I realized how vastly different their world was from mine. Tom, the VP of personnel who leads the team that recruits new missionaries (like a sales team), was presenting his department's goals and strategy for the next year. After spending about twenty minutes walking through how they intended to identify potential new missionaries, communicate the features and benefits of the agency to them, and process their applications, he summed up his remarks by saying that he really could not be held accountable for any of this, because only God can work in someone's heart to draw them into missions.

That quickly, he let his team off the hook. He and his team knew that they could just keep the plates spinning as they always had, and if the people did not show up and they did not meet the goals, the monkey was on God's shoulders. From an entrepreneur's perspective, this gutted the entire planning process and undermined the need to continually work to understand the organization's customer and reinvent ourselves so that we could address those needs—all without changing the corporate mission of reaching the lost around the world.

Of course, it is only through the work of the Spirit of God that someone becomes a missionary—but at the same time, the Bible gives many examples of how we are accountable for how we invest what God has given us. The story of the ten talents is just one good example. God wants us to think and plan wisely and to continually reassess where we are seeing results, and, in response, to reallocate resources—not just hide them in the ground because we fear to take a risk. To hear a mission executive say that he believed he could not be held accountable to numeric goals for his recruitment team put into words one of the great gaps in our respective cultures.

Finding common ground to work with people who think so differently from you is hard work. It would have been easier for me to go back to doing real estate deals with people who understood me and who I understood. At times I felt as though these people had to be from a different planet, and how I wished I could return to my own native people group of hard-driving business entrepreneurs.

Neil served as the chairman of the board for the organization. He spent his days working as a senior executive with Ford

Motor Company, so he understood both cultures. He is wired much like me. With the wisdom that comes from being twenty years older than I am, however, he could see my disconnect. One day he took me aside and told me that he could understand my feelings. He saw how my aggressiveness was blowing fuses in the organization. He understood that I had left a lot of money on the table by giving of my time and talent to the mission instead of spending that time developing real estate. He acknowledged that it appeared my contribution was misunderstood and undervalued. Than he said something that I did not like hearing, but which rang true, even as the words came out of his mouth. "You have every excuse to go back to building more buildings," he said, "but I know you don't want to do that. You don't want to invest the rest of your life in building buildings that will some day be torn down and trucked off to a landfill site. So if you want to make an impact for God around the world through this organization, then you had better suck it up and figure out how."

He was right. And it will likely be the same story for you.

As you encounter this culture gap, remember that the ministry or nonprofit culture is not wrong, and neither is the business culture; but they are different. Both are important and have important strengths. If you try to morph into thinking and acting just like a person who has been in ministry all of his life, you will not bring all the value you could to the team. And if the nonprofit world loses sight of the cause and the values that make it distinct in ministering to the needs of people, that would also be a loss. You need to understand the gap and communicate openly about it so that a greater measure of grace gets shown by all when you are on different wavelengths.

Simply knowing that these differences are likely to exist and committing to talking about them goes a long way toward enabling business and professional leaders to bring their leadership talents to ministries without either getting derailed by the cultural differences or causing significant damage to the organization.

A great way to open discussion in this area is to understand that there are three primary realms in which you operate within a ministry: the Relational; the Organizational; and the Missional. While they operate at the same time in overlapping circles, at times one aspect needs to dominate. Some situations need a large relationship component, while at other times a formal, seemingly cold-hearted organizational focus has to take over. At other times the mission of the organization needs to be the driving force.

The management team at church, for example, often has to make an organizational decision that affects staff. As a family of faith, we are working hard to build a genuine sense of community based on loving and authentic relationships. These two aims can appear to conflict when it comes time to talk with a staff person about performance or his or her role from an organizational perspective. You may not have encountered such a dynamic in your business or professional life. Chances are that if you are the principal of a public school or chief of staff at a hospital, you focus more on organizational and mission issues than on creating a loving sense of family.

To help bridge that gap, I have found it helpful to say at the beginning of such a conversation, "As a leader, I sometimes have to take my relationship hat off and put on my organizational hat. Based on that, we need to make the following changes." This enables both individuals to categorize their interaction and talk corporately while recognizing that the valuable relational aspect of the discussion will have to take place at another time.

At times the mission of the organization needs to dominate over its organizational needs. It will be a big help if you have language that enables you to make this shift clear.

In the final analysis, God is more interested in who we are becoming than in what we accomplish for him. This journey of understanding those we will serve alongside—men and women who have spent their lives in ministry—can be a tool for inner growth and an opportunity for God's remarkable grace to triumph. I have been working alongside the mission organization for ten years now and have come to know and love those folks like family. We often smile and joke about the tough transition I experienced, but that process has helped to pave the way for many others in Halftime who want to join that organization.

Chapter 20

Reengineering Your Niche in the Second Half

By its very nature, Halftime is a process, a journey. It is not an event or a decision, although for me it involved many events and decisions along the way.

Many of us go through this intense period of self-assessment and realignment in our forties or fifties, when we make major structural changes. As you move into your second half of life and engage in whatever God has called you to do, however, your midlife journey continues to evolve—and you will undoubtedly need to reengineer your niche.

The niche you play in your family as grandmother or grandfather will evolve as you discover your best role and posture. Your role as caregiver to your aging parents will evolve as their needs increase. Your role in ministry may need a major overhaul two years into the experience.

In his book *The Seasons of a Man's Life*, Daniel Levinson charts what he believes to be the eras of a healthy man's life. He draws an interesting distinction between what he calls Early Adulthood (ages twenty-two to forty) and Middle Adulthood (ages forty-five to sixty). Sandwiched in between is a five-year span he calls Midlife Transition (from age forty to forty-five). That's the time many of us experience Halftime. Levinson makes a key observation about a Middle Adulthood process he calls Adult Individuation: the task of discovering "who I am in a unique sense." This is the journey of reengineering your second half after you have worked the plan for several years.[1]

This is particularly important for women entering their second half. Studies of how women move through midlife present a somewhat different journey. Richard Olson, in his book *Midlife Journeys: A Traveler's Guide,* summarizes the work of Joanne Vickers and Barbara Thomas in their book *No More Frogs, No More Princes.* There appears to be a dramatic difference between the comfortable, linear approach men take (as described by Levinson) and that which many women take.

After asking more than a hundred women in their forties, fifties, and sixties about their midlife transition, Vickers and Thomas reported that "twenty of the persons they interviewed had found ways to make creative choices for the rest of their lives." In other words, they went through Halftime and began to pursue what they believed would make their second half significant.

They found that the creativity chosen by these women fell into three categories. The first group chose a traditional outlet in arts—for example, painting or pottery—to express themselves. Creativity through art also helped the individual get in touch with her identity, which was a source of great joy.

The second group—the majority—became involved in new work and/or new affiliations. This might be marriage, volunteer work or a new career. These people found a new sense of personal power and fulfillment in these relationships or tasks.

The third group focused on developing their inner lives. Their focus was to create a life that is inner-directed, that is, spiritual. They arranged lifestyles, they allowed time for silence and reflection. For them, creativity is as much letting go as it is taking on new ventures.

Olson asks,

How does one go about making creative choices? Vickers and Thomas interpreted the experiences of the people they interviewed through a paradigm from *The Creative Spirit* by Daniel Goleman, Paul Kaufman, and Michael Ray. This paradigm consists of four stages:

- It begins with preparation. For women, this preparation may begin with the awareness that the relationships in which she has invested herself all her life are coming to be less fulfilling. Something else is needed to make life rich and meaningful. An awareness of physical limitations may dawn upon her as well, bringing a sense of urgency.

- Next there is an incubation. Information and experiences sink into the unconscious, where they grow into new ideas and images. This process just happens. There is nothing that can be done to make it work. Waiting is essential to well-being.

- Incubation is followed by illumination. This may seem to be very sudden—an "aha!" moment, a bolt out of the blue. Actually, it emerges from the two previous processes. This moment of illumination can both delight and frighten a person. It can heighten one's dissatisfaction with life as it is, but it can force one's attention on the need for changes in one's life.

- Finally, there is translation. Out of this self-discovery and realization, the person takes risks to translate dreams into reality.[2]

Translation is the process we are talking about—translating dreams into reality. The dream that your second half of life can be filled with more than just the creative, artistic fulfillment that Vickers and Thomas found many women pursued; more than just turning inward to your own spiritual development, as others in their study did; but going beyond both of those—

turning their hearts outward to discover over time their role in God's plan to redeem this world.

The Vickers and Thomas work helps us to understand the incubation process. Their studies suggest that "Incubation" of your significant second half "just happens" and you cannot play an active role in it or quicken it. They claim that "Illumination" for these women came all of a sudden, as the result of inner processing.[3]

I believe that all of us can do at least two things in this Incubation stage that will impact the Illumination in a healthy way:

- Seek the direction of the Spirit of God
- Seek godly counsel

During your Halftime journey you have made a best effort to understand your gifts and passions and to define what contribution you can best make. But as you move into your second half in the new roles you define for yourself, you will once again have to circle back and refine your roles to craft an even better fit. This is normal.

On the simplest level, as time goes by, what felt exciting for you in the beginning may become routine, so you move to something more exciting and with more variety—you can continue to make choices along the way, and there are many forks in the road.

On a more reflective level, many of us live our first half of life molded into a form designed around others' expectations of us. Many of us have worn masks for forty years that we are just now becoming confident enough to remove. Once we break out of those molds and remove those masks during the Halftime process, our emerging natural tendencies may surprise us. It will take time to come to grips with them. That's part of reengineering your niche.

I discovered, for example, that I am introverted. That is, I gain energy by being and working alone. Crowds of people put an emotional drain on me. That doesn't mean that I don't like being with people or that I am awkward or unsociable in crowds. Not at all. In my first-half career, it was essential that I learn how to interact with people in many settings, including representing our proposed development projects in public city meetings. As a result, I unknowingly squeezed my introverted self into that mold and masked the implications. I refused to acknowledge that long periods of time with people emotionally drained me. I squelched my need for solitude. Three years after I made a Halftime transition, I circled back around and recrafted a set of serving roles that provided me with large chunks of time for solitude.

After you break out of the molds and remove the masks, it takes time to come back to equilibrium. The disruption of Halftime goes deeper than just finding a second-half assignment. It often involves a change in our self-understanding. Some dreams from our first half need to die because they did not really fit us. We will gradually reintegrate this new understanding and find equilibrium.

Most people do not find the best fit on their first try because it takes time before one can begin to assess the impact he or she is making. After a few years, it will become all too apparent that while in one arena you are adding outstanding value, in another role (that really seemed to fit!), your real contribution is marginal at best.

It is almost always through doing that we discover how to refine our niche. Most of us try two or three serving opportunities in our second half before we find a comfortable and sustainable blend. After two or three years of ministry involvement, I found that I had learned a lot about how I can best contribute to an organization.

As I learned more about the role I play best, I sought input from mentors to once again realign my efforts to make my second half as full of impact as possible. I discovered that I needed to be involved in multiple organizations, because my greatest area of contribution, thought leadership, is very narrow. Through involvement in several groups, I could be very intense in my work with one organization for a short period of time, knowing that I could give them time to absorb what I was developing as I worked with the other organization.

I found that, while I need to focus most of my time on strategy development and thought leadership, I also need enough life-on-life serving to keep my heart engaged. Without personally touching people's lives, I found that my heart and passion soon began to wane.

In my initial role in ministry, as the director of communications, I spent most of my time understanding the target audiences, crafting communications strategies and marketing programs to encourage people to become a part of what God was doing around the world. That involves an array of strategic thinking and creative work—developing ideas for literature, website development, video and public relations campaigns. For me it was fun.

After several years of that kind of work, I was thrilled as I began to see the impact I was having on the organization. But I felt that I was miles removed from helping to change any single individual's life. While the piece of work fit me well, the model for doing it kept me too distant from individuals whose lives were benefiting.

The ministry allowed me to renegotiate how I allocated my time, and I began to invest more at church. In church I encounter individuals every week whose lives God is changing through our efforts. One of the highlights of my past five years has been leading Seeker Small Groups. We are constantly offering a small group experience for non-Christians to explore faith in an atmosphere where it is okay to ask tough questions.

About twenty weeks of the year, I lead a Monday night intense discussion among a new group of individuals who are actively exploring Jesus. These groups of five to ten spiritual seekers meet once a week for six weeks. During that time, many of them will ask Jesus to be their leader and forgiver. They often catch up with me months later in the lobby of the church and thank me for the part I played in their journey to God. It thrills me to watch them getting baptized. And it always will.

This new blend of life-on-life ministry was missing from my first iteration of how my second half would look—and that's okay.

This learning comes only with time and by testing the waters. The resulting reinvention of myself in ministry has lead to five of the most enjoyable and fruitful years of ministry. Strangely, you cannot fast track this process. You cannot avoid it by better planning. You cannot cover this ground ahead of time.

In his book, *The Creative Age: Awakening Human Potential in the Second Half of Life*, Dr. Gene Cohen, director of the Center on Aging, Health, and Humanities at George Washington University, draws some very interesting conclusions after years of studying people in midlife. First, he suggests that there are four phases in the second half of life: The Midlife Reevaluation phase in our forties to early sixties (that's Halftime); a Liberation phase in our sixties, with a sense of "If not now, when?"; a Summing-Up Phase, where we find the larger meaning in the story of our lives; and for some, an Encore Phase that affirms life and takes care of business.

Cohen describes the Midlife Reevaluation Phase as:

A time that creative expression is shaped by a sense of crisis or quest. Although midlife crisis is the phrase we hear so often, most adults in this phase actually are motivated by quest-energy to make their life or work more gratifying. Midlife is a powerful time for the expression of human potential because it combines the capacity for insightful reflection with a powerful desire to create meaning in life. This phase typically occurs in those between their forties and early sixties.[4]

He concludes that all these phases "require the passage of time. Midlife Reevaluation isn't something you can work ahead on at age twenty-six."

Cohen writes,

High on the list of those obstacles, at least at midlife, is the fear of time slipping away, the dread of time spent trapped in the 'dark woods' of aging, or simply a sense of time as the enemy, a force that works against us....There is no question that our capacity to experiment remains strong not just despite our age....We need to embrace the passage of time as an asset, an opportunity, a framework for accomplishments and dreams as we age.[5]

Bob Buford says that God has leveled the playing field for us all in that it doesn't matter how smart or how much money we have, we all have a limited time on earth which is slipping away at the very same rate.

Put simply, it takes time for your second-half journey to materialize. You need to be patient enough to let it simmer.

Chapter 21

Discovering That Significance
Was Not Enough

Friday, the week of my fortieth birthday, I found myself flying home after being away for five days. A national disaster earlier that week made air travel slow and unreliable. I could see this would be a long and uncontrollable trip, so I decided to use the entire day, while linking from car to plane to plane to car, to focus my thoughts on one thing: documenting the blessings of God in my life over the past forty years.

I began with a blank sheet of paper and spent the whole day filling that sheet with all the wonderful things I have enjoyed in life and which I so often take for granted. As I scribbled down random thoughts, my list grew. Parents who love and honor God and taught me the Bible from the time I was an infant. A great education. My lovely wife and children. Things we own. Places I have traveled. Adventures I have experienced. Health. Forgiveness.

Have you ever stopped to really focus on all of God's blessings to you? I felt completely overwhelmed with a sense of gratitude for all the ways he has ambushed me with his goodness. Undeserved goodness. Sure, there have been times of suffering and loss. But honestly, as I looked back over my shoulder at the first half of my life and replayed the videos in my mind, I have to admit I have been ambushed by God's goodness. Perhaps most keenly, that day I reexperienced the thrill of finding success in my real estate development career. Many people struggle all their life and never seem to rise above the crowd in anything. I had to pause and thank God for giving me the abilities, the energy, the health, and circumstances to be successful. I remembered the sense of exhilaration when my first residential home development got approved, when the bank agreed to fund our first retirement facility. The sense of pride and accomplishment as I visited our buildings and saw those seniors having a great time, living in the places we dreamed up.

Then I thought about being able to spend part of my time doing things that I consider truly significant. Ten years ago, I had longed to be able to do things that will outlast my short life here on earth. I have been blessed to be able to do just that. God opened up doors to enable me to make a difference in the lives of hundreds of people. What a blast!

My list grew longer and longer. Each entry I wrote brought back memories, and each memory forced my heart to weigh what, of all God's blessings, I value the most. It was a no-brainer that my family was the most valuable thing. I also found it very easy to conclude that, despite the thrill of success and the abiding sense of accomplishment, pursuing eternal significance is far better than my first-half definition of success.

But where my thoughts ended that day came as a complete surprise. When I managed to shut out the clutter of airport noise—waiting for boarding passes, moving between terminals, dealing with frustrating delays—down at the core of my being, I valued most of all those brief moments when my heart found complete satisfaction in God himself.

It dawned on me that I had set out on a journey from success to significance—only to find that significance alone could never fill the emptiness in my heart. What I was really longing for all along was satisfaction.

Not the satisfaction that comes from success, achievements, and acquisition; that's transient. Not the satisfaction that comes from using your talents to make an impact on others—even though that is eternal. Rather, I desired most deeply of all the satisfaction of doing life with God in an all-out pursuit of his honor and glory—to willingly let God use me for large or small impact, as he saw fit.

That day I realized that the most satisfying moment of my forty years had not come at some island beach resort. Not during a ribbon-cutting ceremony of a grand new building. Not even the proud moment when my first child, Carter, was born. No. It had been a single moment, standing out in a hot parking lot with a few people milling around—but a moment when my heart connected, *really* connected, with the living God.

And I was satisfied.

I stood in the parking lot, looking up at a new building I had helped build—but a different kind of building this time . . . our church building. The school we were renting had abruptly canceled our lease, forcing us to build a 26,000-square-foot structure in less than a hundred days.

Our media team captured each day's work on film as the structure emerged out of the ground almost overnight. Now, when I watch it, it seems the closest thing I know of to a videotaped miracle. Leading that project was the craziest, yet most energizing thing I have ever done. At each step of the project I knew that if God did not show up, it would absolutely fail. For example, normally, you can't even get preengineered steel delivered in a hundred days, much less build a complete building from the ground up.

This day occurred five years and three months after the ribbon-cutting ceremony at Huntington Green, when I experienced my "two-minute warning"—but this was a very, very different day. Against all odds, the city's chief building inspector overruled our site inspector and granted our occupancy permit, the day before we had to leave the school. God had shown up all through this project, and now he showed up in such an unmistakable way that I realized this project had been God's project all along, and that I merely had the privilege of walking alongside him.

In one brief moment that Friday afternoon, I looked up into the sky and realized at the deepest soul level that God had chosen me to partner with him to build a facility where hundreds of people will come and discover a relationship with him. I felt as if my heart touched the heart of God—an indescribable thrill, if even for a moment.

Success has been a blast. Pursuing eternal significance has been far more rewarding, eternally rewarding.

But my heart wanted satisfaction more than anything else.

Ultimately, this satisfaction comes only as we walk with God, where he is going, using our time, talent, and resources at his beck and call and experiencing him at an increasingly deep level along the way.

It's about availability, not ability. It's about options, not affluence.

It's about desiring God above all else.

For one-on-one coaching through
your Halftime journey, email Lloyd at
Lloyd.Reeb@halftime.org

Explore the Halftime Institute and other powerful tools at
www.halftime.org and *www.LloydReeb.com*

Notes

Foreword by Bob Buford

1. Gregg Easterbrook, *The Progress Paradox: How Life Gets Better While People Feel Worse* (New York: Random House, 2003), xix.

Chapter 1

1. Fawn M. Brodie, *Thomas Jefferson: An Intimate History* (New York: Bantam, 1974), 344, 360. Also: Jefferson's letter to Madison, June 9, 1793, from Thomas Jefferson, *Writings*, L. and B. IX, 118–19.

Chapter 3

1. Elisabeth Elliot, *These Strange Ashes* (San Francisco: Harper & Row, 1975), 28, 129.

Chapter 9

1. Dr. Richard A. Swenson, *Margin* (Colorado Springs, Colo.: NavPress, 2002), 91.

Chapter 16

1. Ideas from Tom McGehee in *Whoosh* (Cambridge, Mass., Perseus Publishing, 2001).
2. The story of Jim and Connie Phillips is used by permission from Fellowship Bible Church, Little Rock, Arkansas.

Chapter 20

1. Daniel Levinson, Charlotte N. Darrow, Edward B. Klein, Maria H. Levinson, and Brazton McKee, *The Seasons of a Man's Life* (New York: Alfred A. Knopf, 1978), 19.

2. Richard Olson: *Midlife Journeys, A Traveler's Guide* (Cleveland: Pilgrim Press, 1996), 28–30.
3. Joanne Vickers and Barbara Thomas, No More Frogs, *No More Princes: Women Making Creative Choices at Midlife* (Freedom, Calif.: Crossing Press, 1993), 7–8.
4. Gene D. Cohen, *The Creative Age* (New York: Avon, 2000), 78, 116.
5. Ibid.